100 POP HITS OF THE '90s

arranged by Dan Coates

Project Manager: *Carol Cuellar*
Cover Design: *Jorge Paredes*

CONTENTS

4

From Walt Disney's "BEAUTY AND THE BEAST"

BEAUTY AND THE BEAST

Words by
HOWARD ASHMAN

Music by
ALAN MENKEN
Arranged by DAN COATES

Slowly, with expression

Beauty and the Beast - 4 - 1

Theme from "UP CLOSE & PERSONAL"

BECAUSE YOU LOVED ME

Words and Music by
DIANE WARREN
Arranged by DAN COATES

12

Because You Loved Me - 5 - 5

BUTTERFLY KISSES

Words and Music by
BOB CARLISLE and RANDY THOMAS
Arranged by DAN COATES

Butterfly Kisses - 5 - 1

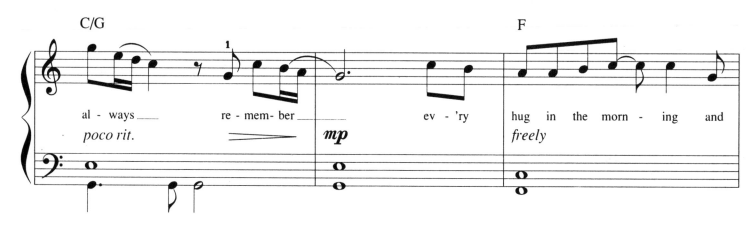

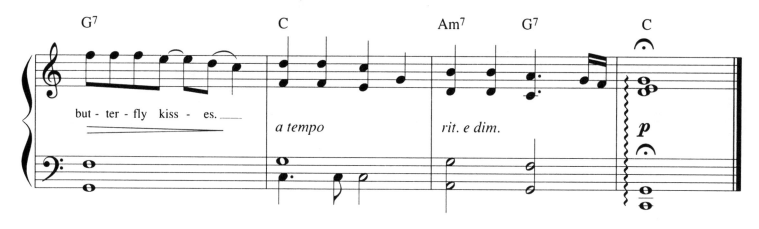

Verse 2:
Sweet sixteen today,
She's lookin' like her mama a little more every day.
One part woman, the other part girl;
To perfume and make-up from ribbons and curls.
Trying her wings out in a great big world.
But I remember:

Chorus 2:
Butterfly kisses after bedtime prayer,
Stickin' little white flowers all up in her hair.
"You know how much I love you, daddy, but if you don't mind,
I'm only gonna kiss you on the cheek this time."
Oh, with all that I've done wrong, I must have done something right
To deserve her love every morning
And butterfly kisses at night.

Verse 3:
She'll change her name today.
She'll make a promise, and I'll give her away.
Standing in the brideroom just staring at her,
She asks me what I'm thinking, and I say, "I'm not sure.
I just feel like I'm losing my baby girl."
Then she leaned over and gave me...

Chorus 3:
Butterfly kisses with her mama there,
Stickin' little white flowers all up in her hair.
"Walk me down the aisle, daddy, it's just about time."
"Does my wedding gown look pretty, daddy? Daddy, don't cry."
Oh, with all that I've done wrong, I must have done something right
To deserve her love every morning
And butterfly kisses. *(Coda)*

From the Motion Picture "POETIC JUSTICE"

AGAIN

Written by
JANET JACKSON,
JAMES HARRIS III and TERRY LEWIS
Arranged by DAN COATES

Moderately Slow

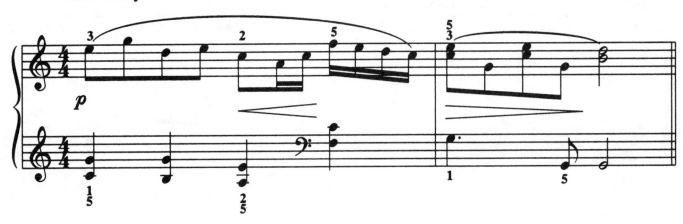

I heard from a friend to - day and she said you were in town. Sud - den -

ly the mem - o - ries came back to me in my mind._____ How can

Again - 4 - 1

ALL THE MAN THAT I NEED

Words and Music by
DEAN PITCHFORD and MICHAEL GORE
Arranged by DAN COATES

All the Man That I Need - 4 - 1

ALWAYS AND FOREVER

Words and Music by
ROD TEMPERTON
Arranged by DAN COATES

Always and Forever - 3 - 1

ANGEL EYES

Composed by
JIM BRICKMAN
Arranged by DAN COATES

Angel Eyes - 3 - 1

Angel Eyes - 3 - 3

ALWAYS BE MY BABY

Words and Music by
MANUEL SEAL, JERMAINE DUPRI
and MARIAH CAREY
Arranged by DAN COATES

Always Be My Baby - 4 - 1

Now you want to be free,_____ so I'll let you fly._____
But in - ev - i - ta - bly,_____ you'll be back a - gain._____

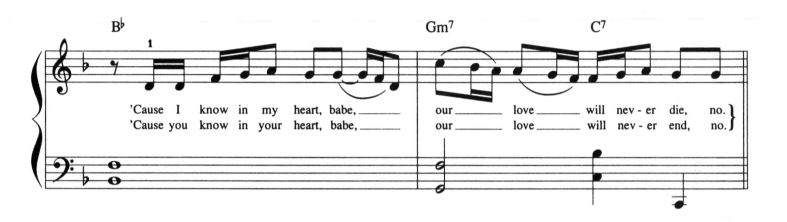

'Cause I know in my heart, babe,_____ our_____ love_____ will nev - er die, no.}
'Cause you know in your heart, babe,_____ our_____ love_____ will nev - er end, no.}

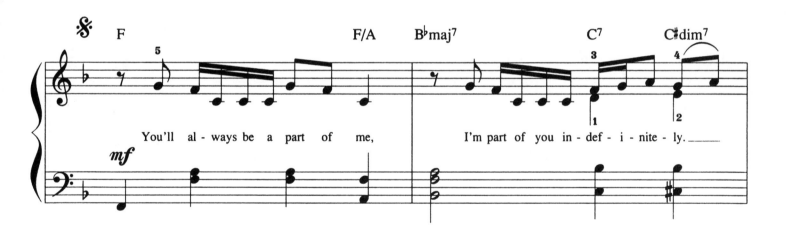

You'll al - ways be a part of me, I'm part of you in - def - i - nite - ly._____

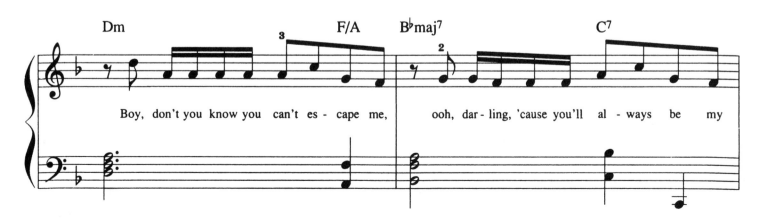

Boy, don't you know you can't es - cape me, ooh, dar - ling, 'cause you'll al - ways be my

ANGELS AMONG US

Words and Music by
BECKY HOBBS and DON GOODMAN
Arranged by DAN COATES

Additional lyrics

Spoken: *When life held troubled times and had me down on my knees*
There's always been someone to come along and comfort me.
A kind word from a stranger, to lend a helping hand,
A phone call from a friend just to say I understand.
Sung: *Now, ain't it kind of funny, at the dark end of the road,*
Someone lights the way with just a single ray of hope.
(To Chorus)

BY HEART

Composed by
JIM BRICKMAN and
HOLLYE LEVEN
Arranged by DAN COATES

By Heart - 3 - 1

BREAKFAST AT TIFFANY'S

Words and Music by
TODD PIPES
Arranged by DAN COATES

Verse 2:
I see you, the only one who knew me,
But now your eyes see through me.
I guess I was wrong.
So what now?
It's plain to see we're over,
I hate when things are over,
When so much is left undone. *(To Chorus:)*

Verse 3:
You'll say we got nothing in common,
No common ground to start from,
And we're falling apart.
You'll say
The world has come between us,
Our lives have come between us,
Still I know you just don't care. *(To Chorus:)*

From Walt Disney's "THE LION KING"

CAN YOU FEEL THE LOVE TONIGHT

Lyrics by
TIM RICE

Music by
ELTON JOHN
Arranged by DAN COATES

48

From Walt Disney's "POCAHONTAS"

COLORS OF THE WIND

Lyrics by
STEPHEN SCHWARTZ

Music by
ALAN MENKEN
Arranged by DAN COATES

Colors of the Wind - 4 - 1

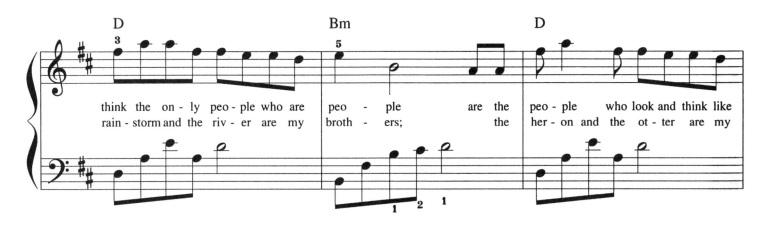

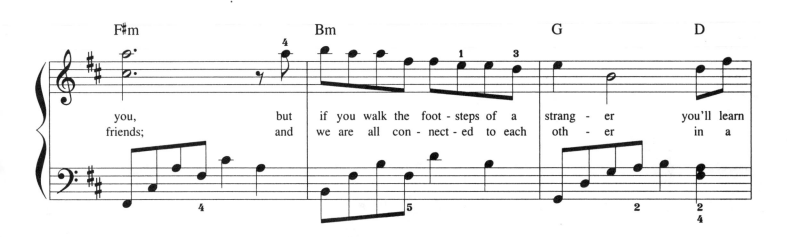

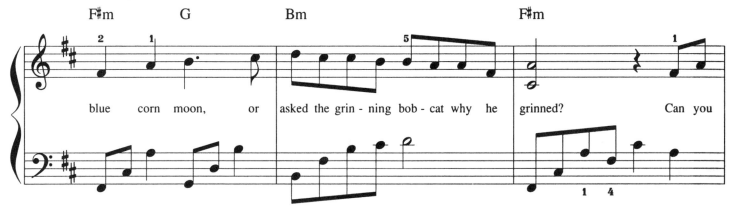

Colors of the Wind - 4 - 2

COME TO MY WINDOW

Lyrics and Music by
MELISSA ETHERIDGE
Arranged by DAN COATES

Moderately slow ♩ = 76

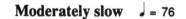

mf Come to my win - dow. ___ Crawl in - side, wait by the light ___ of the

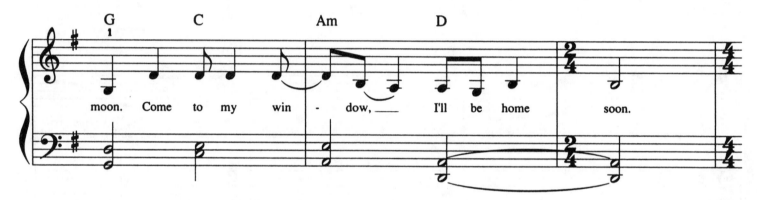

moon. Come to my win - dow, ___ I'll be home soon.

Faster ♩ = 92

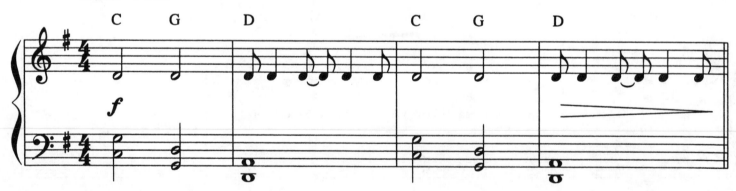

mf I would dial the num - bers just to lis - ten to your breath. And

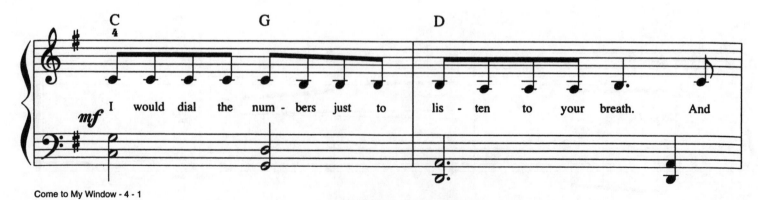

Come to My Window - 4 - 1

D.S. 𝄋 al Coda

𝄉 Coda

Verse 2:
Keeping my eyes open, I cannot afford to sleep.
Giving away promises I know that I can't keep.
Nothing fills the blackness that has seeped into my chest.
I need you in my blood, I am forsaking all the rest.
Just to reach you,
Just to reach you.
Oh, to reach you. *(To Chorus:)*

COMPLETELY

Words and Music by
DIANE WARREN
Arranged by DAN COATES

Slowly, with expression

Com - plete - ly ____ wan - na give my love, com - plete - ly. ____ I'd ra - ther be a - lone than be in love just half the way. I want to find some - one that I can trust com -

Completely - 5 - 1

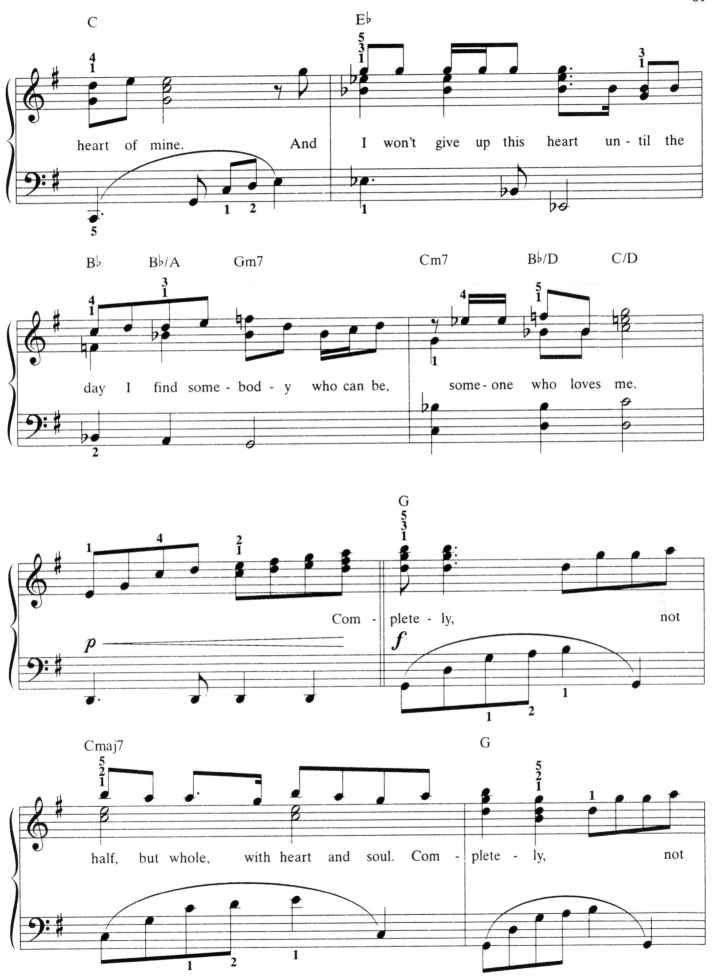

COUNT ON ME

Words and Music by
BABYFACE, WHITNEY HOUSTON
and MICHAEL HOUSTON
Arranged by DAN COATES

Count on Me - 5 - 1

DREAMING OF YOU

Words and Music by
TOM SNOW and FRANNE GOLDE
Arranged by DAN COATES

1. Late at night when all the world___ is sleep-ing, I stay up and think of you.___

4. Late at night when all the world___ is sleep-ing, I stay up and think of you.___

And I wish on a star___ that some-where you are___ think-ing

And I still can't be-lieve___ that you came up to me___ and said,

of me, too.___ 'Cause I'm dream - ing___ of

"I love you." ___ I love you, too.___ Now, I'm dream - ing___ with

Dreaming of You - 4 - 1

from WAITING TO EXHALE

EXHALE
(Shoop Shoop)

Words and Music by
BABYFACE
Arranged by DAN COATES

75

Exhale - 4 - 4

From the Twentieth Century Fox Motion Picture "ONE FINE DAY"

FOR THE FIRST TIME

Words and Music by
JAMES NEWTON HOWARD,
ALLAN RICH and JUD FRIEDMAN
Arranged by DAN COATES

For the First Time - 5 - 1

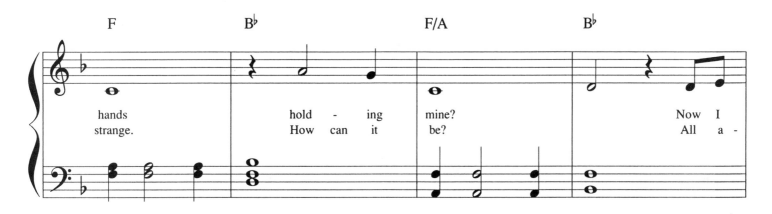

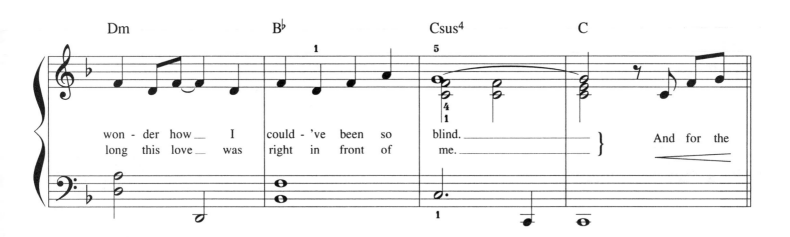

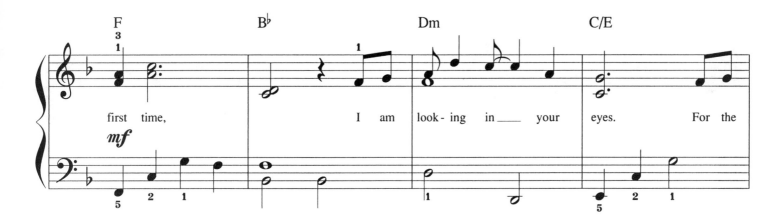

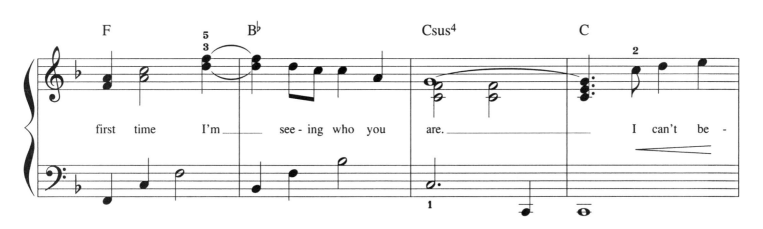

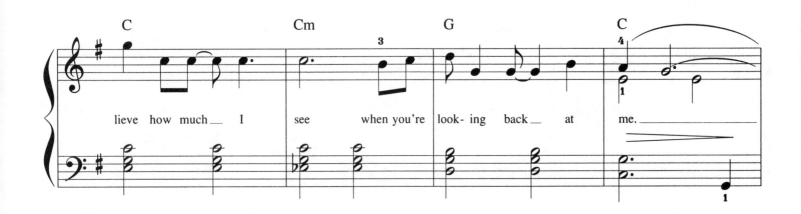

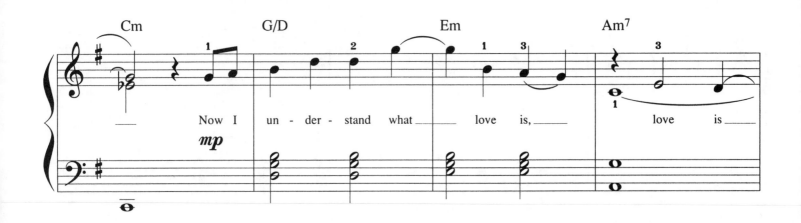

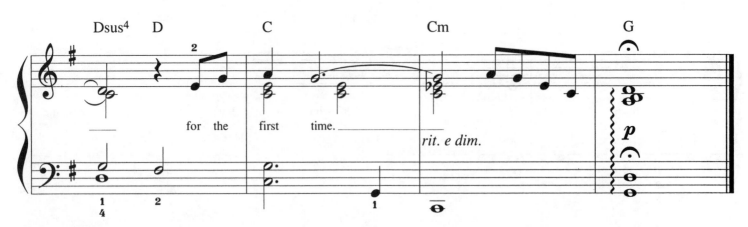

FOREVER

Words and Music by
MICHAEL BOLTON
and PAUL STANLEY
Arranged by DAN COATES

Forever - 5 - 1

I lived my life be-liev-ing all love is blind,— but

ev-'ry-thing a-bout you is tell-ing me this time

it's for-ev-er.—

This time I know and there's no doubt in my mind,— for-

FOR YOU

Words and Music by
KENNY LERUM
Arranged by DAN COATES

For You - 4 - 1

Coda

you.

Ev - 'ry - thing I do now makes sense,

all roads end. All I do is for you,

on - ly for you.

rit. e dim.

Verse 2:
For you, I share the cup of love that overflows,
And anyone who knows us knows
That I would change all thoughts I have for you.
There is no low or high or in-between
Of my heart that you haven't seen.
'Cause I share all I have and am.
Nothing I've said is hard to understand.
All I feel, I feel deeper still and always will.
All this love is for you.

Verse 3:
For you, I make a promise of fidelity,
Now and for eternity.
No one could replace this love for you,
I take your hand and heart and everything,
And add to them a wedding ring.
'Cause this life is no good alone,
Since we've become one, you're all I know.
If this feeling should leave, I'd die.
And here is why, all I am is for you.

FOR YOU I WILL

Words and Music by
DIANE WARREN
Arranged by DAN COATES

Moderately slow ♩ = 72

Verse:

1. When you're feel - ing lost in the night, _____ when you feel your

world just ain't right, _____ call on me, I will be wait - ing. Count on

me, I will be there. An - y - time the times get too tough, _____ an - y - time your

best ain't e - nough, _____ I'll be the one to make it bet - ter.

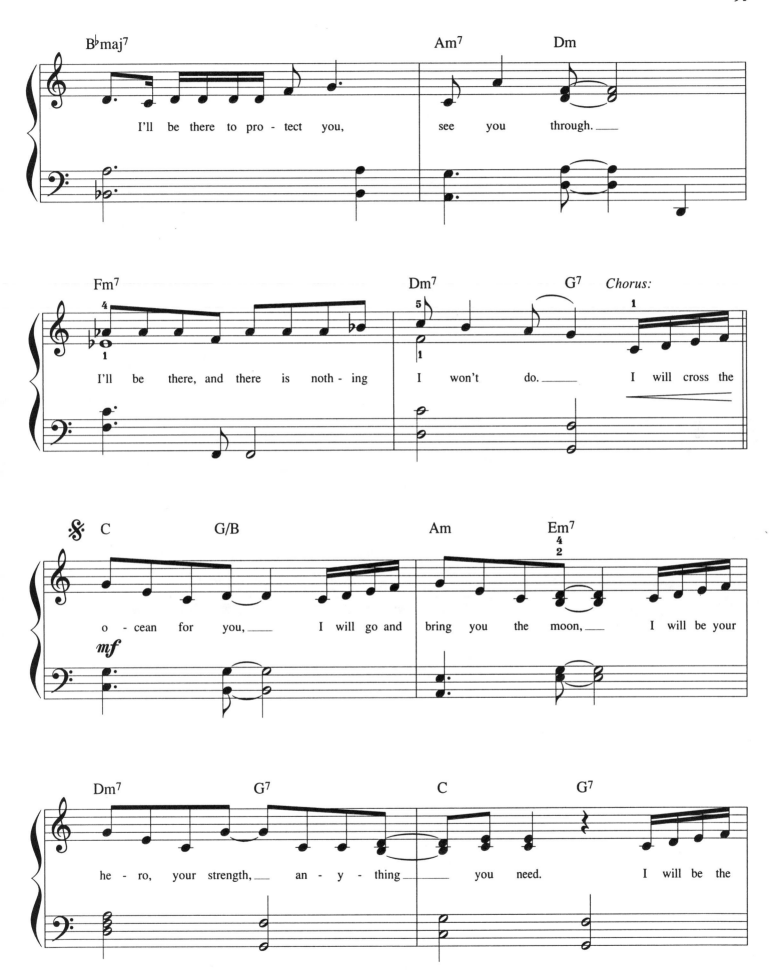

D.S. 𝄋 al Coda

give my word, I'll give it all. Put your faith in me, I'll do an-y-thing. I will cross the

Coda

will. Prom - ise you, for you I

will. I prom - ise you, for you I will.

rit. e dim.

Verse 2:
I will shield your heart from the rain,
I won't let no harm come your way.
Oh, these arms will be your shelter,
No, these arms won't let you down.
If there is a mountain to move,
I will move that mountain for you.
I'm here for you, I'm here forever.
I will be a fortress, tall and strong.
I'll keep you safe, I'll stand beside you,
Right or wrong.   *(To Chorus:)*

GET HERE

Words and Music by
BRENDA RUSSELL
Arranged by DAN COATES

Slowly

You can reach me by rail - way,__ you can reach me by
sail - boat,__ climb a tree and swing
(See additional lyrics)

Trail - way.__ You can reach me on an air - plane,__ you can
rope to rope.__ Take a sled and slide down slope__ in -

(simile)

Get Here - 4 - 1

Extra Lyrics:

You can windsurf into my life,
Take me up on a carpet ride.
You can make it in a big balloon
But you better make it soon.

You can reach me by caravan,
Cross the desert like an Arab man.
I don't care how you get here,
Just get here if you can.

From the Original Motion Picture Soundtrack "DON JUAN DeMARCO"

HAVE YOU EVER REALLY LOVED A WOMAN?

Lyrics by
BRYAN ADAMS and
ROBERT JOHN "MUTT" LANGE

Music by
MICHAEL KAMEN
Arranged by DAN COATES

Have You Ever Really Loved a Woman? - 4 - 1

HEAL THE WORLD

Written and Composed by
MICHAEL JACKSON
Arranged by DAN COATES

Moderately Slow

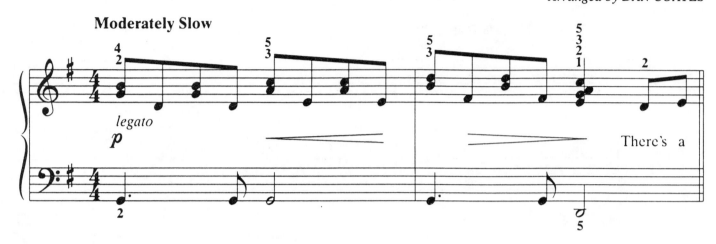

legato
p
There's a

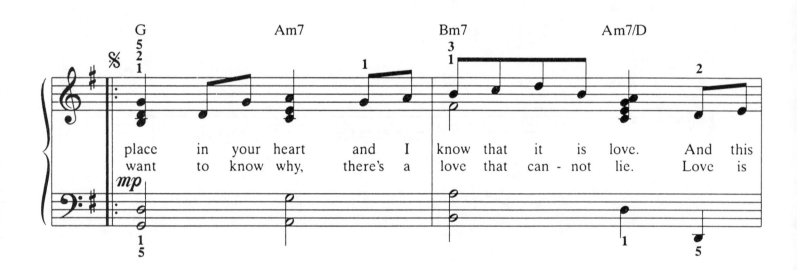

G Am7 Bm7 Am7/D

mp

place in your heart and I know that it is love. And this
want to know why, there's a love that can - not lie. Love is

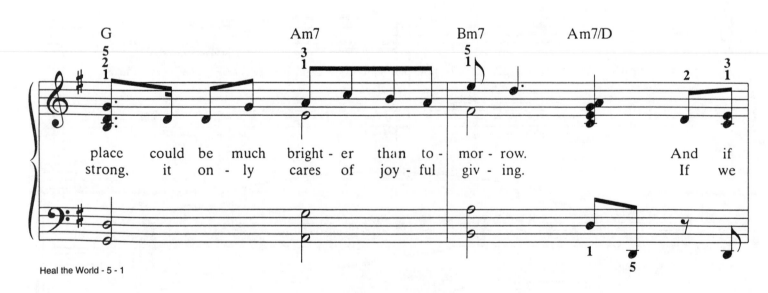

G Am7 Bm7 Am7/D

place could be much bright - er than to - mor - row.   And if
strong, it on - ly cares of joy - ful giv - ing.   If we

Heal the World - 5 - 1

106

Extra Lyrics:

We could fly so high,
Let our spirits never die.
In my heart, I feel
You are all my brothers.
Create a world with no fear,
Together we cry happy tears.
See the nation turn
Their swords into plowshares.
We could really get there,
If you cared enough for the living.
Make a little space
To make a better place.
(Chorus)

HOW DO YOU TALK TO AN ANGEL

By
STEVE TYRELL,
STEPHANIE TYRELL and BARRY COFFING
Arranged by DAN COATES

How Do You Talk to an Angel - 5 - 1

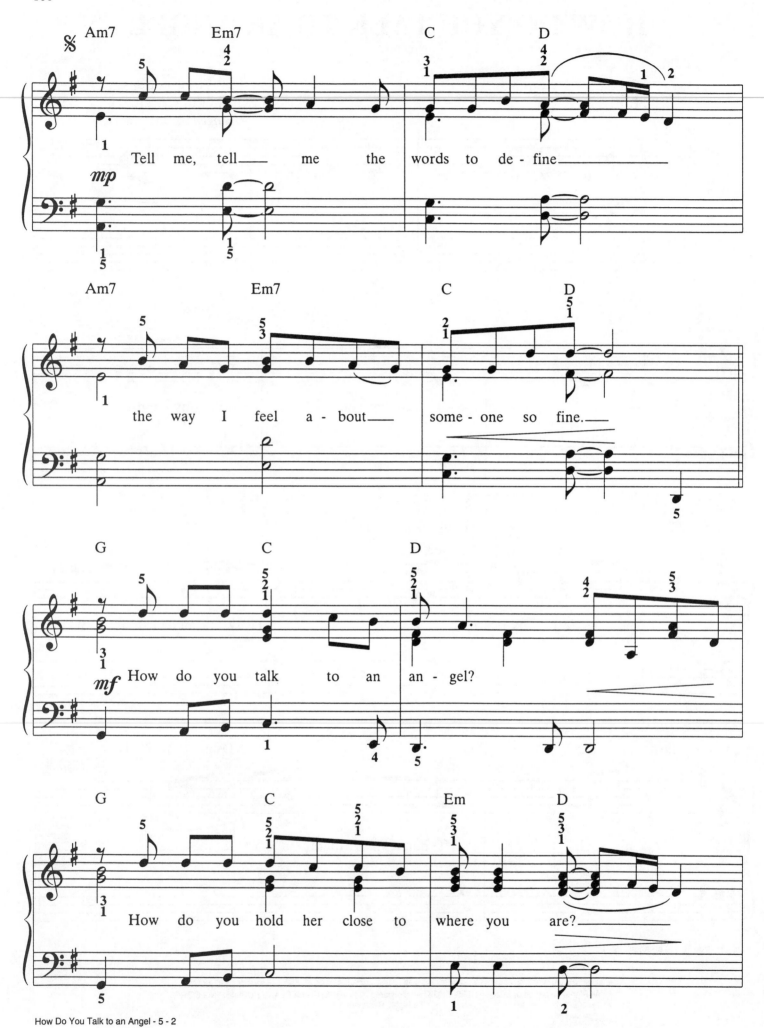

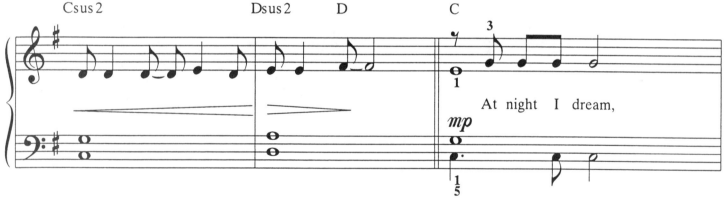

How Do You Talk to an Angel - 5 - 3

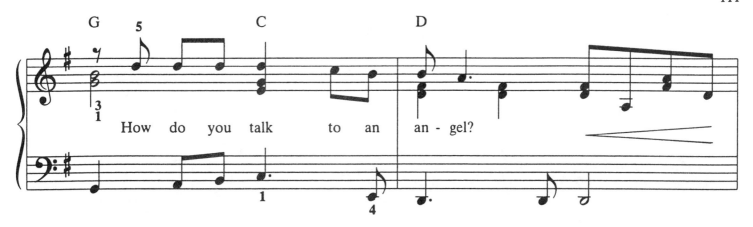

How do you talk to an an - gel?

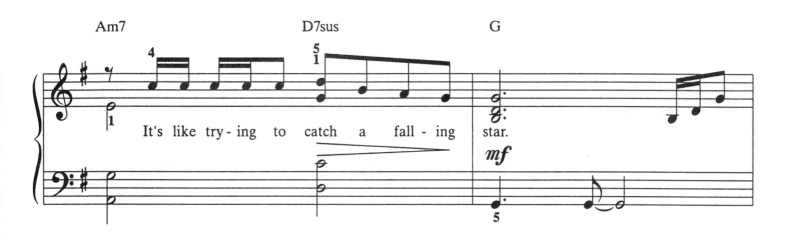

It's like try - ing to catch a fall - ing star.

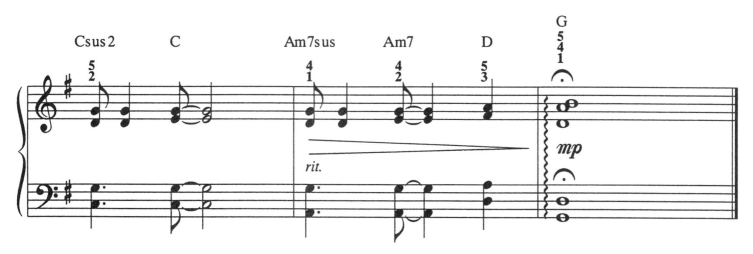

How Do You Talk to an Angel - 5 - 5

HERO

Words and Music by
WALTER AFANASIEFF
and MARIAH CAREY
Arranged by DAN COATES

Hero - 4 - 1

113

Hero - 4 - 2

HERO'S DREAM

Composed by
JIM BRICKMAN
Arranged by DAN COATES

Hero's Dream - 4 - 1

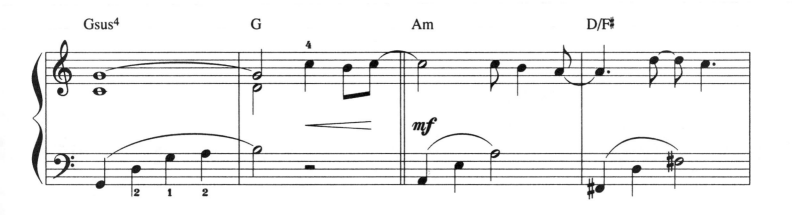

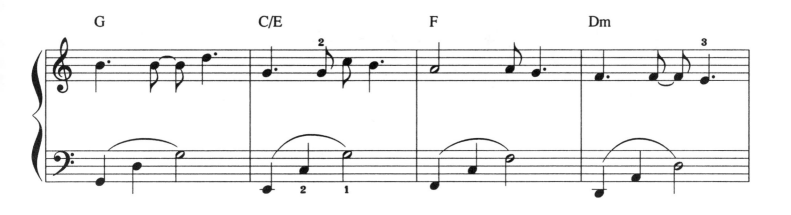

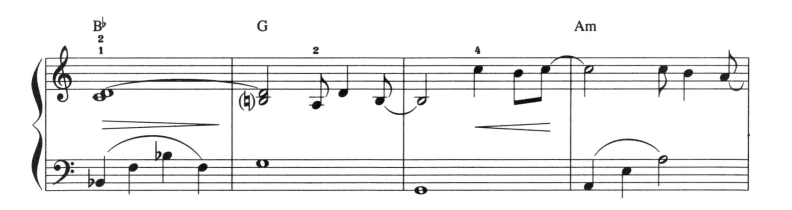

Hero's Dream - 4 - 2

HOLD ME, THRILL ME, KISS ME

Words and Music by
HARRY NOBLE
Arranged by DAN COATES

Hold Me, Thrill Me, Kiss Me - 4 - 4

HOUSE OF LOVE

Words and Music by
GREG BARNHILL, KENNY GREENBERG
and WALLY WILSON
Arranged by DAN COATES

Moderate rock beat

House of Love - 4 - 1

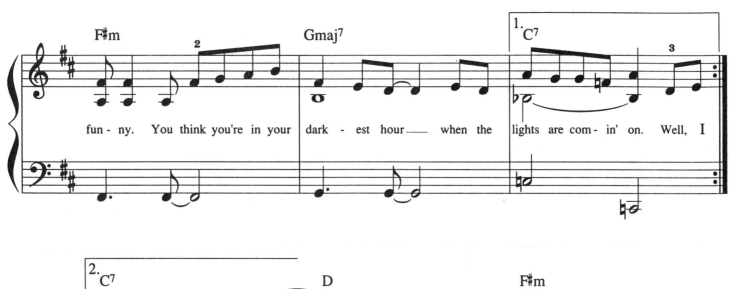

fun - ny. You think you're in your dark - est hour — when the lights are com - in' on. Well, I

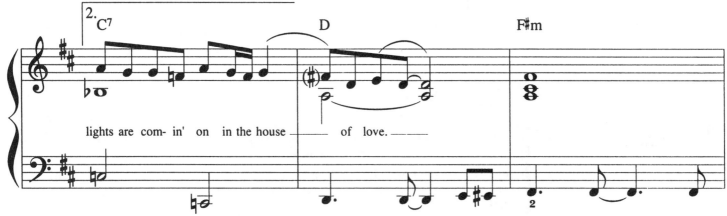

lights are com- in' on in the house — of love. —

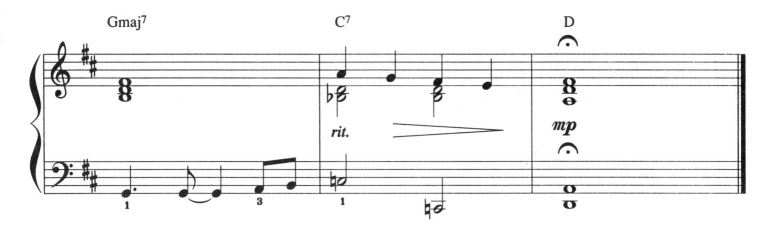

Verse 2:
Now, when the house is dark and you're all alone inside,
You've gotta listen to your heart, put away your foolish pride.
Though the storm is breakin' and thunder shakes the walls,
There with a firm foundation ain't it never, never, never gonna fall.
(To Chorus:)

Verse 3:
Though the storm is breakin' and thunder shakes the walls,
There with a firm foundation ain't it never, never, never gonna fall.
(To Chorus:)

I BELIEVE I CAN FLY

Words and Music by
R. KELLY
Arranged by DAN COATES

I Believe I Can Fly - 4 - 1

From the Motion Picture "THE PREACHER'S WIFE"
I BELIEVE IN YOU AND ME

Words and Music by
SANDY LINZER and DAVID WOLFERT
Arranged by DAN COATES

I Believe in You and Me - 4 - 1

134

Verse 2:
I will never leave your side,
I will never hurt your pride.
When all the chips are down,
I will always be around
Just to be right where you are, my love.
Oh, I love you, boy.
I will never leave you out,
I will always let you in
To places no one has ever been.
Deep inside, can't you see?
I believe in you and me.

I CAN LOVE YOU LIKE THAT

Words and Music by
STEVE DIAMOND, MARIBETH DERRY
and JENNIFER KIMBALL
Arranged by DAN COATES

Moderately slow

(with pedal)

1. They read you Cin-der-el-la, you
nev-er make a pro-mise I

hoped it would come true, ___ that
don't in-tend to keep, ___ so

one day your Prince Charm-ing would come ___ res-cue you. ___ You
when I say for-ev-er, for-ev-er's what I mean.

like ro-man-tic mov-ies, you
I'm no Ca-sa-no-va, but I

nev-er will for-get the
swear this much is true:

way you felt when Ro-me-o kissed
I'll be hold-ing noth-ing back when

I Can Love You Like That - 4 - 1

From the Warner Bros. Film "PURE COUNTRY"

I CROSS MY HEART

Words and Music by
STEVE DORFF and ERIC KAZ
Arranged by DAN COATES

I Cross My Heart - 5 - 1

Additional Lyrics

2. You will always be the miracle
   That makes my life complete.
   And as long as there's a breath in me
   I'll make yours just as sweet.
   As we look into the future,
   It's as far as we can see.
   So let's make each tomorrow
   Be the best that it can be.
   (To Chorus)

I DO

Words and Music by
PAUL BRANDT
Arranged by DAN COATES

Verse 3:
I know the time will disappear,
But this love we're building on will always be here.
No way that this is sinking sand,
On this solid rock we'll stand forever.
(To Chorus:)

I Do - 3 - 3

From the Motion Picture "ROBIN HOOD: PRINCE OF THIEVES"

(EVERYTHING I DO) I DO IT FOR YOU

Written by
BRYAN ADAMS, ROBERT JOHN "MUTT" LANGE
and MICHAEL KAMEN
Arranged by DAN COATES

(Everything I Do) I Do It for You - 5 - 1

150

I DON'T WANT TO

Words and Music by
R. KELLY
Arranged by DAN COATES

From the Motion Picture "THE MIRROR HAS TWO FACES"

I FINALLY FOUND SOMEONE

Written by
BARBRA STREISAND, MARVIN HAMLISCH,
R. J. LANGE and BRYAN ADAMS
Arranged by DAN COATES

I Finally Found Someone - 6 - 1

I LOVE YOU ALWAYS FOREVER

Words and Music by
DONNA LEWIS
Arranged by DAN COATES

I Love You Always Forever - 4 - 1

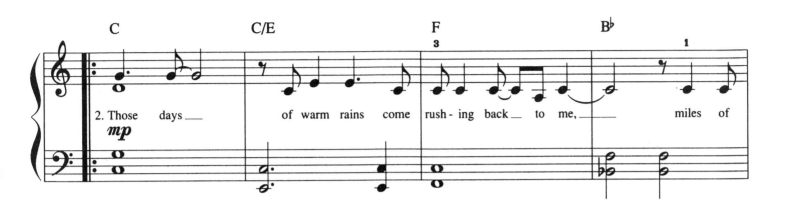

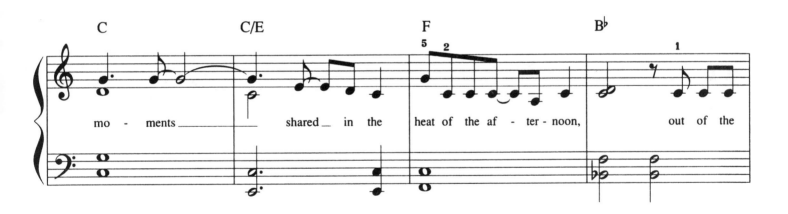

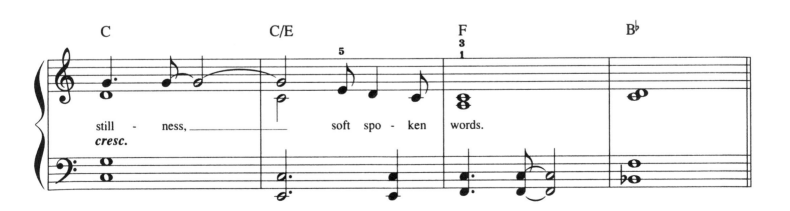

Chorus:

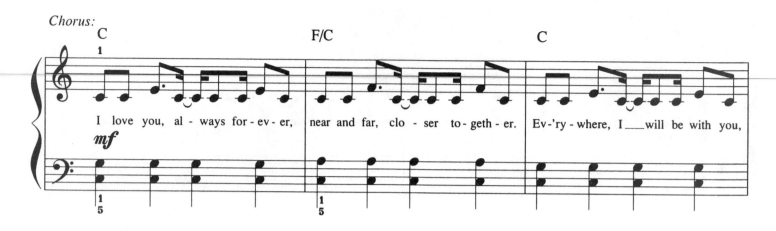

I love you, al - ways for - ev - er, near and far, clo - ser to - geth - er. Ev - 'ry - where, I ___ will be with you,

mf

ev - 'ry - thing, I ___ will do for you. I love you, al - ways for - ev - er, near and far, clo - ser to - geth - er.

Ev - 'ry - where, I ___ will be with you, ev - 'ry - thing, I ___ will do for you. ev - 'ry - thing, I ___ will do for you.

Say you love, love ___ me for - ev - er, nev - er stop, nev - er what - ev - er. Near and far and al - ways and ev - 'ry -

f

Verse 3:
You've got the most unbelievable blue eyes I've ever seen.
You've got me almost melting away as we lay there
Under blue sky with pure white stars,
Exotic sweetness, a magical time.
(To Chorus:)

I SWEAR

Words and Music by
GARY BAKER and FRANK MYERS
Arranged by DAN COATES

I see the ques - tion in___ your eyes,___
I'll give you ev - 'ry - thing___ I can,___

I know what's weigh - ing on___ your mind,___ but you can be sure___
I'll build your dreams___ with these___ two hands,___ and we'll hang some mem-

I Swear - 4 - 1

I WISH IT WOULD RAIN DOWN

Words and Music by
PHIL COLLINS
Arranged by DAN COATES

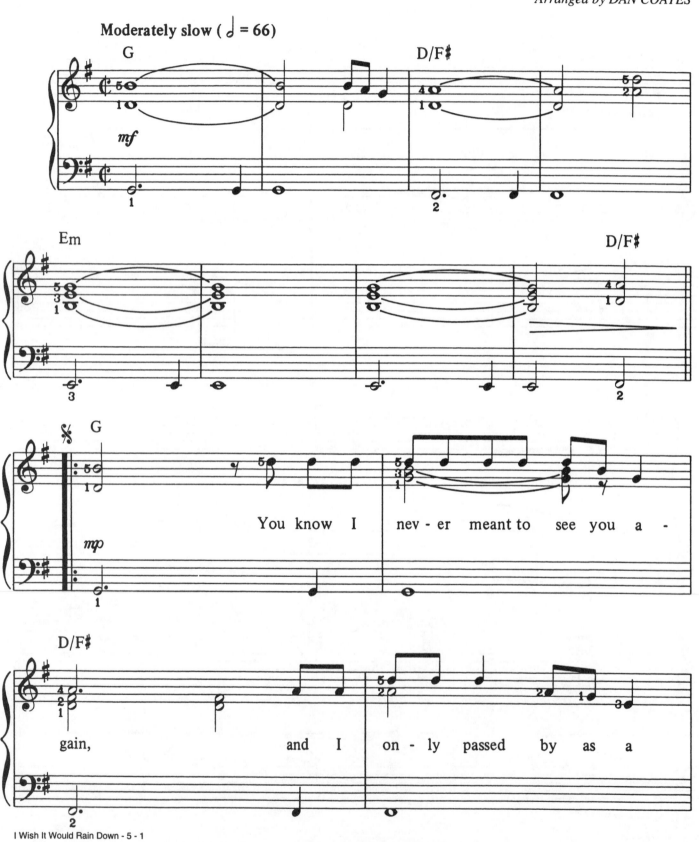

You know I nev-er meant to see you a-gain, and I on-ly passed by as a

I Wish It Would Rain Down - 5 - 1

174

Coda

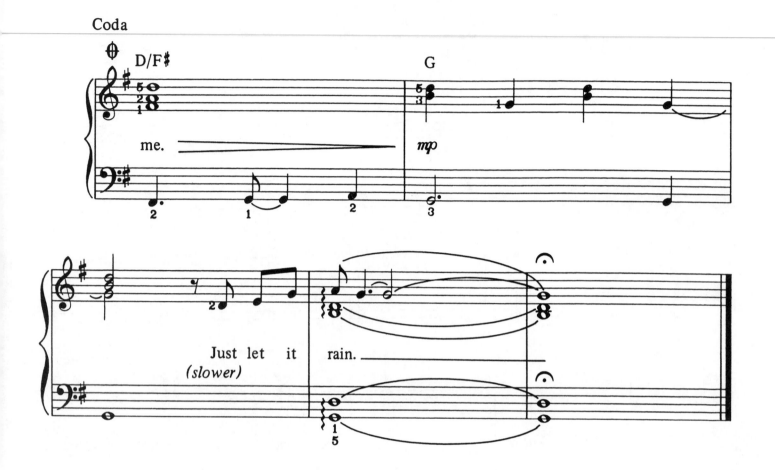

me.

mp

Just let it rain.

(slower)

Additional Lyrics

2. You said you didn't need me in your life,
   Oh I guess you were right,
   Ooh I never meant to cause you no pain,
   But it looks like I did it again.

3. 'Cause I know, I know I never meant to cause you no pain,
   And I realise I let you down,
   But I know in my heart of hearts,
   I know I'm never gonna hold you again.

IF TOMORROW NEVER COMES

Words and Music by
KENT BLAZY and GARTH BROOKS
Arranged by DAN COATES

If Tomorrow Never Comes - 3 - 1

Verse 2:
'Cause I've lost loved ones in my life
Who never knew how much I loved them.
Now I live with the regret
That my true feelings for them never were revealed.
So I made a promise to myself
To say each day how much she means to me
And avoid the circumstance
Where there's no second chance
To tell her how I feel. 'Cause... *(To Chorus:)*

IF YOU ASKED ME TO

Words and Music by
DIANE WARREN
Arranged by DAN COATES

Used to be that I be- lieved in____ some- thing,
Some- how ev - er since I've been a - round____ you

used to be that I be- lieved in love.____
can't go back to be - ing on my own.____

It's been a long time since I've had that feel - ing, I could
Can't help feel - ing, dar - lin', since I've found____ you that I've

If You Asked Me to - 4 - 3

IF YOU GO

Words and Music by
JON SECADA and MIGUEL A. MOREJON
Arranged by DAN COATES

If You Go - 3 - 1

Verse 2:
Sorry if you felt misled
But I know what I feel, I know what I said, baby.
God, I hope you believe, believe in all that we can be,
The future in us together in love.
You're the reason I'm strong.
Don't you think I don't know
This is where I belong?
Give me the time to say that you're mine
To say that you're mine.
(To Chorus:)

IN THIS LIFE

Words and Music by
MIKE REID and
ALLEN SHAMBLIN
Arranged by DAN COATES

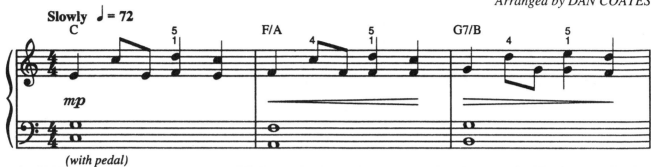

For all I'd been blessed with in my life,

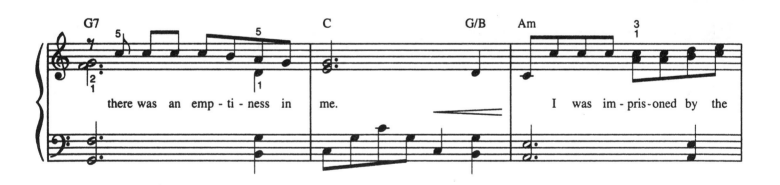

there was an emp-ti-ness in me. I was im-pris-oned by the

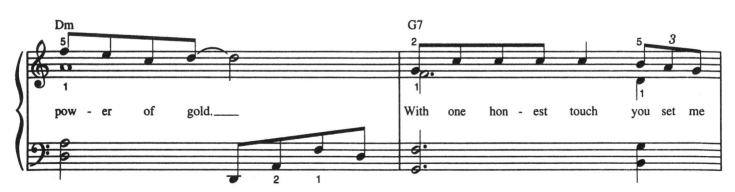

pow - er of gold.___ With one hon - est touch you set me

In This Life - 3 - 1

free. Let the world stop turn - ing, let the

sun stop burn - ing. Let them tell me love's not worth___ go - ing

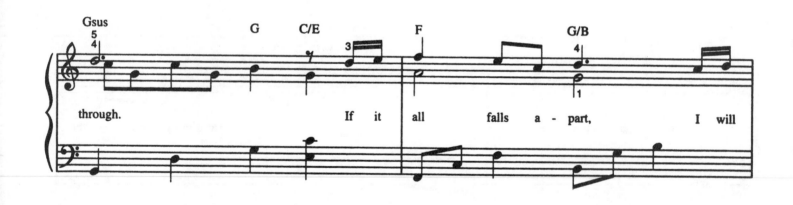

through. If it all falls a - part, I will

know deep in my heart the on - ly dream that mat - tered had come

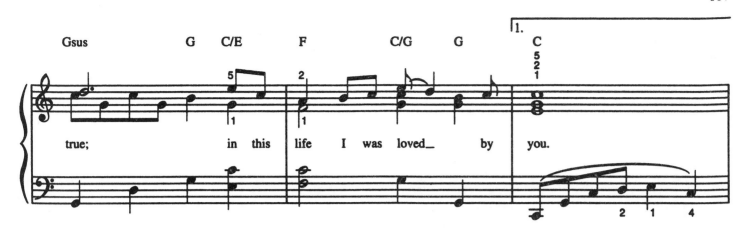

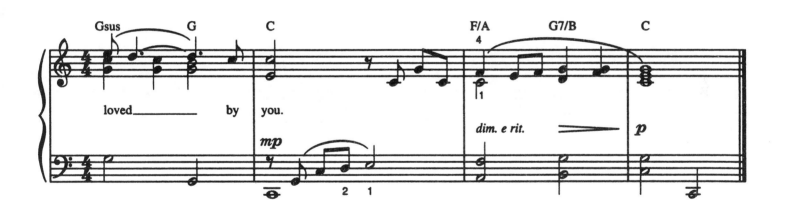

Verse 2:
For every mountain I have climbed,
Every raging river crossed,
You were the treasure that I longed to find.
Without your love I would be lost.
(To Chorus:)

I'D LIE FOR YOU
(And That's the Truth)

Words and Music by
DIANE WARREN
Arranged by DAN COATES

KEY WEST INTERMEZZO
(I SAW YOU FIRST)

Words and Music by
JOHN MELLENCAMP
and GEORGE GREEN
Arranged by DAN COATES

Key West Intermezzo - 5 - 1

194

Verse 3:
On a moon spattered road in her parrot rebozo,
Gypsy Scotty is driving his big, long, yellow car.
She flies like a bird over his shoulder.
She whispers in his ear, "Boy, you are my star."
(To Chorus:)

Verse 4:
In the bone colored dawn, me and Gypsy Scotty are singin',
The radio is playing, she left her shoes out in the back.
He tells me a story about some girl he knows in Kentucky.
He just made that story up, there ain't no girl like that.
(To Chorus:)

I'LL BE THERE FOR YOU
(Theme from "FRIENDS")

Words by
DAVID CRANE, MARTA KAUFFMAN, ALLEE WILLIS,
PHIL SOLEM and DANNY WILDE

Music by
MICHAEL SKLOFF
Arranged by DAN COATES

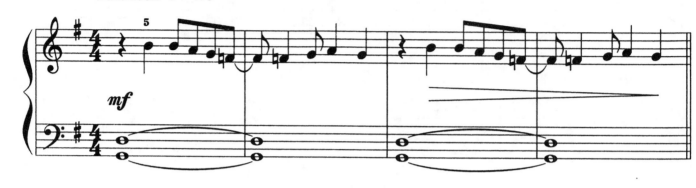

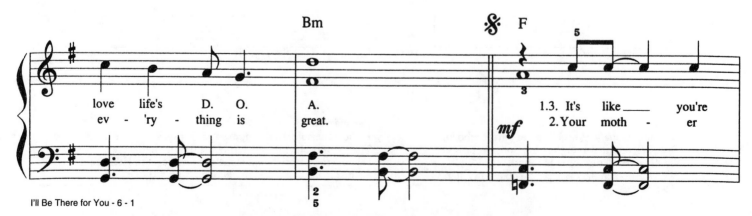

I'll Be There for You - 6 - 1

when the rain starts to fall. I'll be there for you like I've been there be - fore. I'll be there for you 'cause you're there for me, too.

rit. e dim.

mf

I'LL NEVER GET OVER
YOU GETTING OVER ME

Words and Music by
DIANE WARREN
Arranged by DAN COATES

Moderate ballad

I hear you're

tak-ing the town a-gain, hav-ing a good time with all your
smile so the hurt won't show; tell ev-'ry-bod-y that I was glad to

good time friends. I don't think that you think of me, you're on your
see you go. But the tears just won't go a-way, lone-li-ness

own now and I'm a-lone and free. I know that I should get on
found me, looks like it's here to stay. I know that I ought to find

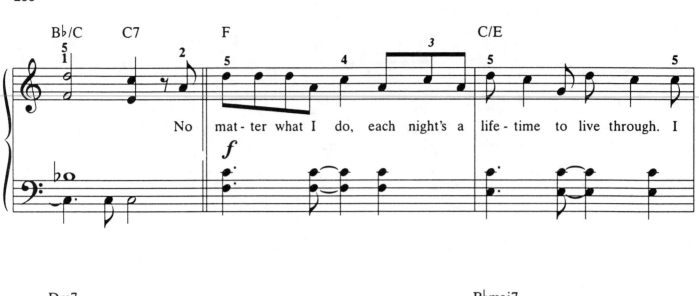

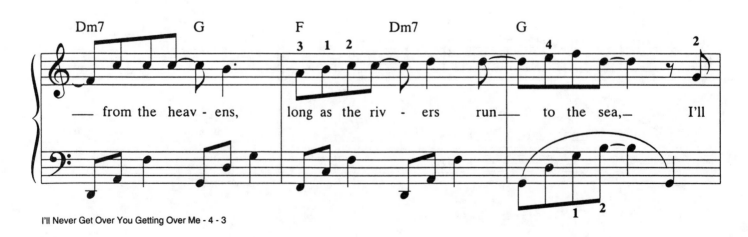

THE KEEPER OF THE STARS

Words and Music by
KAREN STALEY, DANNY MAYO and DICKEY LEE
Arranged by DAN COATES

The Keeper of the Stars - 4 - 1

thanks to the keep - er of the stars. _____

It was no ac - ci - dent, me find - ing you.

Some - one had a hand in it long be - fore we ev - er knew.

dim. e rit.

The Keeper of the Stars - 4 - 4

KILLING ME SOFTLY
(WITH HIS SONG)

Words by
NORMAN GIMBLE

Music by
CHARLES FOX
Arranged by DAN COATES

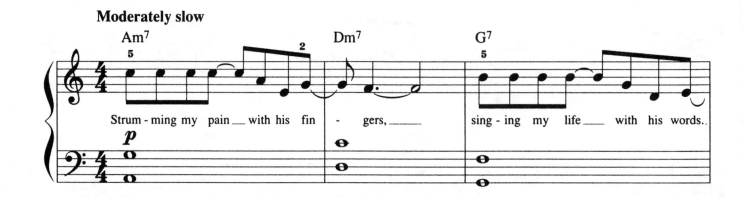

Verse 3:
He sang as if he knew me,
In all my dark despair.
And then he looked right through me
As if I wasn't there.
But he was there, this stranger
Singing clear and strong. *(To Chorus:)*

LANE'S THEME

Composed by
BILL CONTI
Arranged by DAN COATES

Lane's Theme - 3 - 1

LIKE A PRAYER

Words and Music by
MADONNA CICCONE and PAT LEONARD
Arranged by DAN COATES

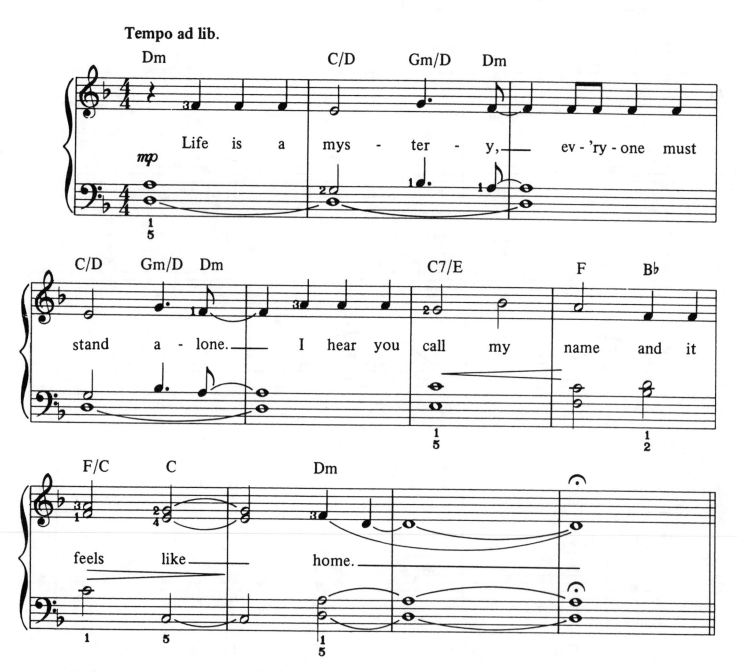

Like a Prayer - 6 - 1

Moderate Dance beat

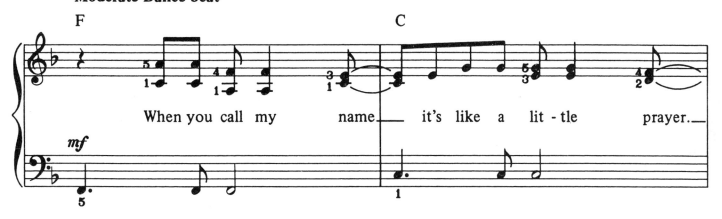

When you call my name___ it's like a lit - tle prayer.___

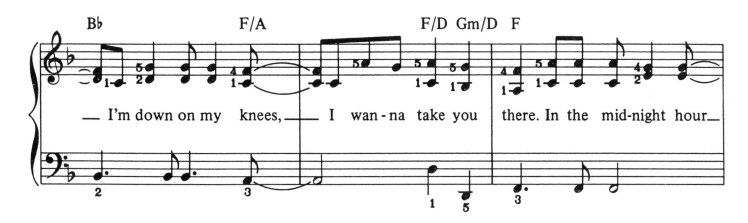

___ I'm down on my knees,___ I wan - na take you there. In the mid-night hour___

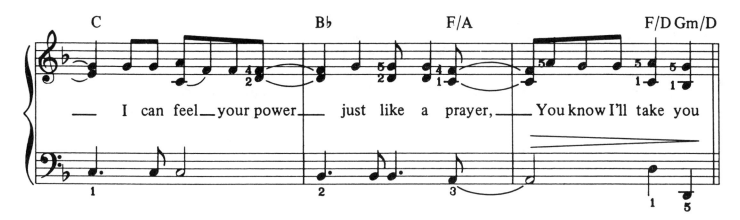

___ I can feel___your power___ just like a prayer,___ You know I'll take you

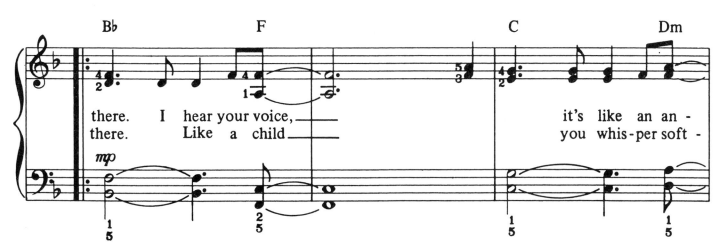

there. I hear your voice,___
there. Like a child___

it's like an an -
you whis-per soft -

THE LIVING YEARS

By
MIKE RUTHERFORD and B.A. ROBERTSON
Arranged by DAN COATES

The Living Years - 4 - 1

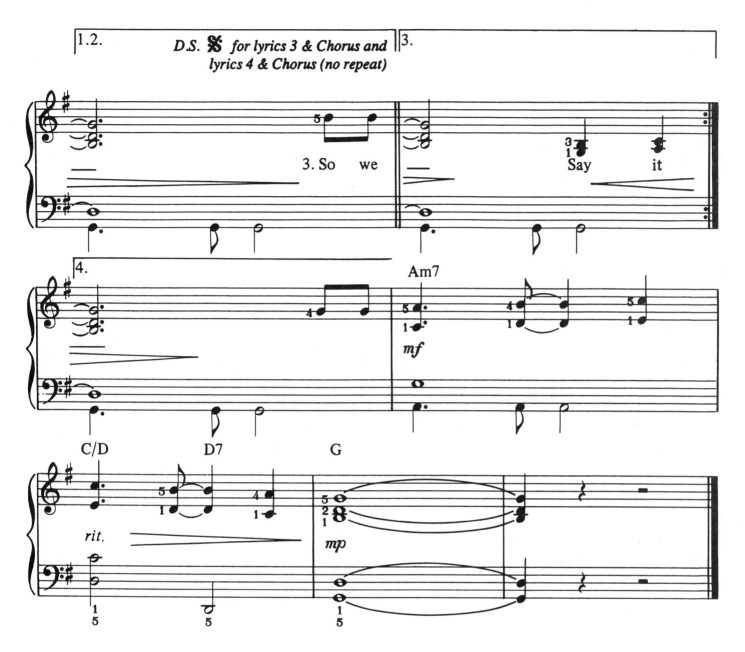

Additional Lyrics

3. So we open up a quarrel
   Between the present and the past.
   We only sacrifice the future,
   It's the bitterness that lasts.
   So don't yield to the fortunes
   You sometimes see as fate.
   It may have a new perspective
   On a different day.
   And if you don't give up, and don't give in
   You may just be O.K.

   Chorus:

4. I wasn't there that morning
   When my father passed away.
   I didn't get to tell him
   All the things I had to say.
   I think I caught his spirit
   Later that same year.
   I'm sure I heard his echo
   In my baby's new born tears.
   I just wish I could have told him
   In the living years.

   Chorus:

LOVE IS

Words and Music by
JOHN KELLER, TONIO K.
and MICHAEL CARUSO
Arranged by DAN COATES

Slowly

p legato

Pedal throughout

Am They say it's a riv - er

A♭+ that cir - cles the earth,

C/G a beam of light shin - ing to the edge

D7/F♯ of the un - i - verse.

Love Is - 6 - 1

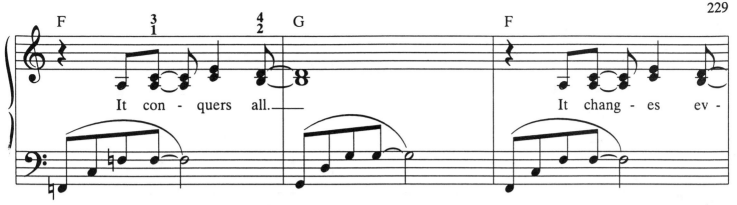

It con - quers all. It chang - es ev -

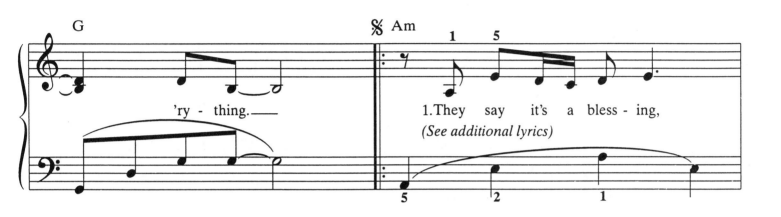

'ry - thing. 1.They say it's a bless - ing,
(See additional lyrics)

they say it's a gift. They say it's a mir - a - cle, and I be -

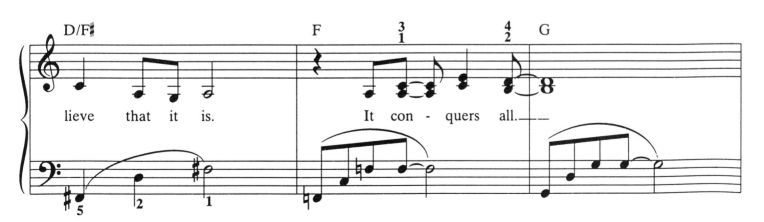

lieve that it is. It con - quers all.

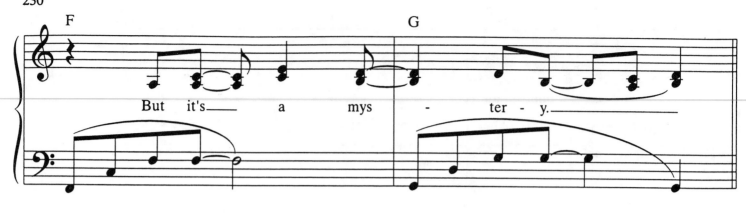

But it's___ a mys - ter - y.___

1.3.Love breaks___ your heart.___ Love takes___ no less___

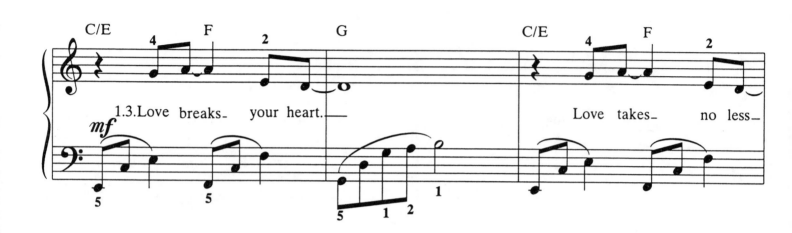

___ than ev - 'ry-thing. Love makes___ it hard,___ and it

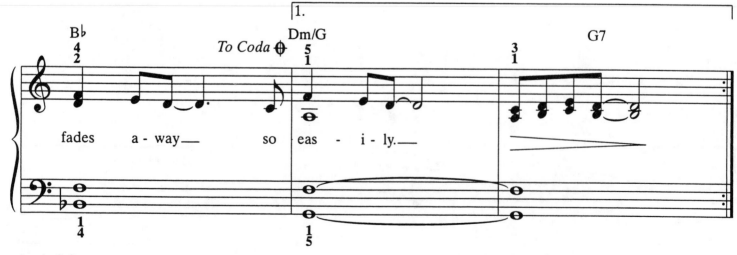

fades a - way___ so eas - i - ly.___

Additional Lyrics:

2. In this world we've created,
   In this place that we live,
   In the blink of an eye, babe,
   The darkness slips in.
   Love lights the world,
   Unites the lovers for eternity.

   Love breaks the chains.
   Love aches for every one of us.
   Love takes the tears and the pain
   And it turns it into
   The beauty that remains.

LOVE IS A WONDERFUL THING

Words and Music by
MICHAEL BOLTON
and ANDY GOLDMARK
Arranged by DAN COATES

Love Is a Wonderful Thing - 5 - 1

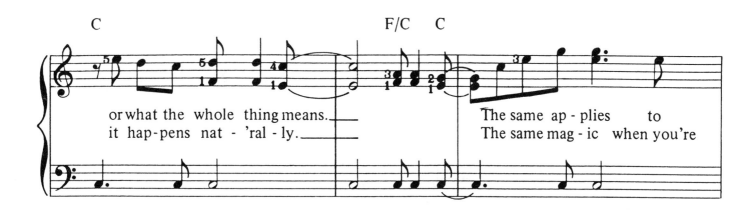

C   F/C   C

or what the whole thing means.____ The same ap - plies   to
it hap - pens nat - 'ral - ly.____ The same mag - ic when you're

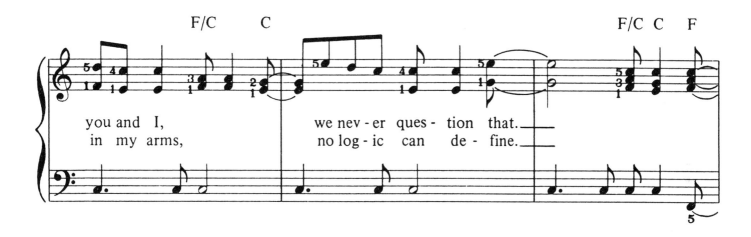

F/C   C   F/C   C   F

you and I,   we nev - er ques - tion that.____
in my arms,   no log - ic can de - fine.____

Am

So   good,   it's   un - der - stood.____
Don't know why,   just   feel   so   right.____

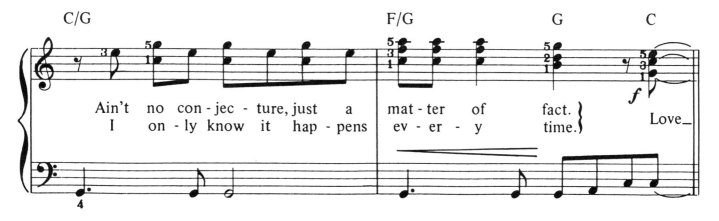

C/G   F/G   G   C

Ain't no con - jec - ture, just   a   mat - ter of   fact. ⎱
I   on - ly know it hap - pens   ev - er - y   time. ⎰

f

Love____

236

To Coda

Dm   F/G   1. C F/C C F/C C

love___ is a won-der-ful thing. *mf*

2.

F/C C   F/C C   C F/C C   F/C C

thing.

Em7   Am7

Oh, when the   cold wind   blows,   I know_you're gon - na

Dm7   C/E

be there to warm   me.   Oh,_ that's what   keeps me   go - in', and

Love Is a Wonderful Thing - 5 - 5

MENTAL PICTURE

Words and Music by
JON SECADA and
MIGUEL A. MOREJON
Arranged by DAN COATES

Mental Picture - 3 - 1

Verse 2:
Time was of the essence,
And as usual the day turns into minutes.
Sharing love and tenderness,
That's the nerve you struck in me that sent a signal.
To the other side,
(Girl, I don't know)
Saying my blind side.
And if a ... *(To Chorus:)*

LOVE WILL KEEP US ALIVE

Words and Music by
JIM CAPALDI, PETER VALE
and PAUL CARRACK
Arranged by DAN COATES

MACARENA

Words and Music by
ANTONIO ROMERO
and RAFAEL RUIZ
Arranged by DAN COATES

Macarena - 4 - 1

grí - a Ma - ca - re - na que tu cuer - po_es pa' dar - le_a - le - grí - a_y co - sa - bue - na.

Da - le_a tu cuer - po_a - le - grí - a Ma - ca - re - na, eh, Ma - ca - re - na. Ma - ca -

G

re - na tie - ne_un no - vio que se lla - ma, que - se lla - ma de_a - pe - lli - do Vi - to -

mp

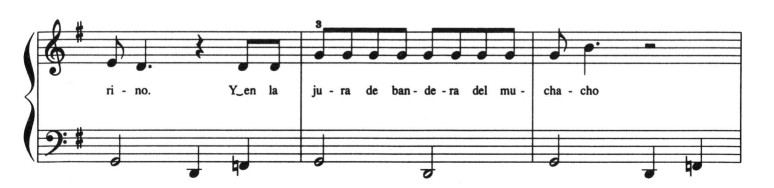

ri - no. Y_en la ju - ra de ban - de - ra del mu - cha - cho

Macarena - 4 - 2

MORE THAN WORDS

Lyrics and Music by
BETTENCOURT, CHERONE
Arranged by DAN COATES

More Than Words - 5 - 1

THE MOST BEAUTIFUL GIRL IN THE WORLD

Composed by

Arranged by DAN COATES

The Most Beautiful Girl in the World - 3 - 2

NOW AND FOREVER

Music and Lyrics by
RICHARD MARX
Arranged by DAN COATES

1. When - ev - er I'm wear - y ____ from the
2. Some - times I just hold you, ____
3. *(Instrumental)*

bat - tles that rage in my head, you make sense of
too caught up in me to see I'm hold - ing a

mad - ness when my san - i - ty hangs by a thread.
for - tune that heav - en has giv - en to me.

Now and Forever - 3 - 1

Now and Forever - 3 - 2

ONE MOMENT IN TIME

Words and Music by
ALBERT HAMMOND and JOHN BETTIS
Arranged by DAN COATES

Slowly, with expression

Each day I live I want to be a day to
heart for ev-'ry gain; to taste the

give the best of me.
sweet, I faced the pain.

I'm on-ly one, but not a-
I rise and fall, yet through it

lone. My fin-est day is yet un-known. I broke my
all this much re-

One Moment in Time - 5 - 1

262

263

One Moment in Time - 5 - 3

264

Extra Lyrics

I've lived to be
The very best.
I want it all,
No time for less.
I've laid the plans,
Now lay the chance
Here in my hands.

From the TriStar Pictures Feature Film "ONLY YOU"

ONCE IN A LIFETIME

Words and Music by
WALTER AFANASIEFF, MICHAEL BOLTON
and DIANE WARREN
Arranged by DAN COATES

Once in a Lifetime - 4 - 1

ONE OF US

Words and Music by
ERIC BAZILIAN
Arranged by DAN COATES

One of Us - 4 - 1

272

OPEN ARMS

Words and Music by
STEVE PERRY and
JONATHAN CAIN
Arranged by DAN COATES

Open Arms - 3 - 1

here _____ I am with o - pen arms, _____ hop - ing to see what your love means to me; o - pen arms.

REACH

Words and Music by
GLORIA ESTEFAN and
DIANE WARREN
Arranged by DAN COATES

1. Some dreams _____ live on in time ___ for- ev- er.
2. Some days _____ are meant to be ___ re- mem- bered.

Those dreams _____ you want with all _____ your
Those days, _____ we rise a- bove _____ the

heart. _____
stars. _____

And I'll
So, I'll

278

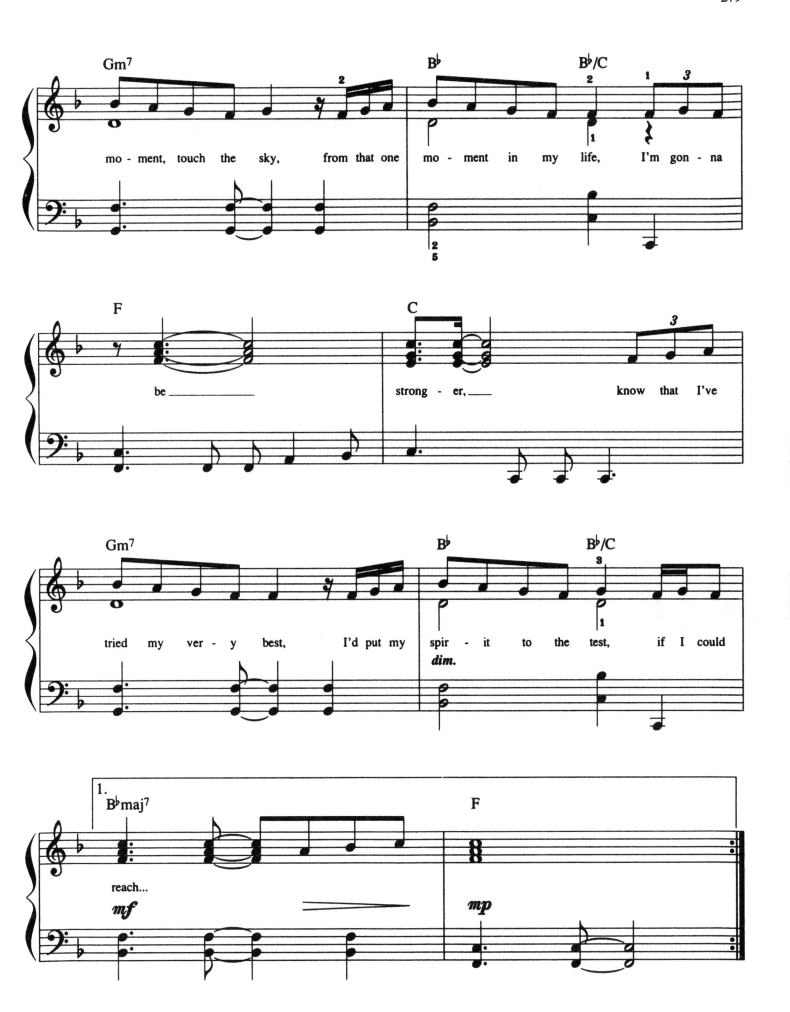

280

Reach - 5 - 4

Inspired by the Columbia Pictures Feature Film "THE PRINCE OF TIDES"

PLACES THAT BELONG TO YOU

Lyrics by
ALAN and MARILYN BERGMAN

Music by
JAMES NEWTON HOWARD
Arranged by DAN COATES

Moderately Slow

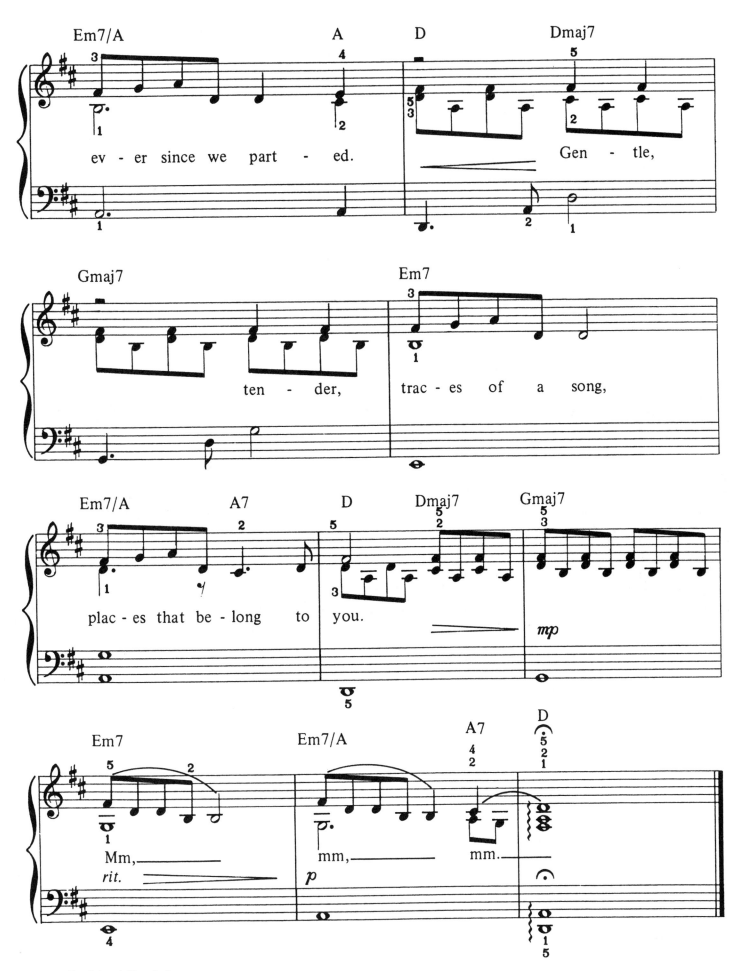

QUIT PLAYING GAMES
(With My Heart)

Words and Music by
MAX MARTIN and HERBERT CRICHLOW
Arranged by DAN COATES

Bright rock tempo

1. Ev - en in my heart life the

see you're not be - ing true to me. Deep with - in my

way to keep you com - in' back to me. Ev - 'ry - thing I

soul I feel no - thing's like it used to

do is for you, so what is it that you can't

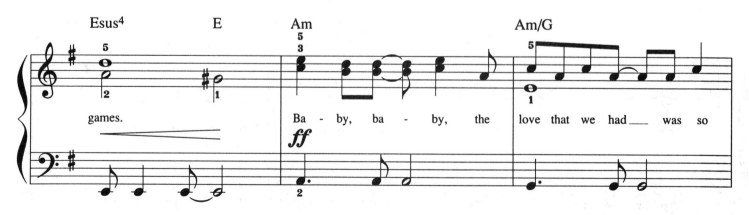

RESTLESS HEART

Words and Music by
ANDY HILL and
PETER CETERA
Arranged by DAN COATES

Moderate, steady beat

I don't wan-na lose you, I__ don't want you walk-in' a-way.__
Tell me where you want me, an-y time, I don't care.__

We're so good to-geth-er, tell__
Tell me when you need me, ba-

__ me it's for-ev-er, 'cause I
by, when you need me, I will

wan-na stay.__
be right there.__

Restless Heart - 4 - 1

THE RIVER

Words and Music by
VICTORIA SHAW and GARTH BROOKS
Arranged by DAN COATES

1. You know a dream is like a riv-er,___ ev-er chang-in' as it flows.___ And the dream-er's just___ a ves-sel___ that must fol-low where it goes.___ Try-ing to

The River - 4 - 1

Verse 2:
Too many times we stand aside
And let the waters slip away
'Til what we put off 'til tomorrow
Has now become today.
So, don't you sit upon the shoreline
And say you're satisfied.
Choose to chance the rapids
And dare to dance the tide.
Yes, I will...   *(To Chorus:)*

SAVE THE BEST FOR LAST

Words and Music by
WENDY WALDMAN, JON LIND
and PHIL GALDSTON
Arranged by DAN COATES

Save the Best for Last - 4 - 1

302

Additional Lyrics

Sometimes the snow comes down in June,
Sometimes the sun goes 'round the moon.
Just when I thought our chance had passed,
You go and save the best for last.

SAY YOU'LL BE THERE

Words and Music by
SPICE GIRLS
and ELIOT KENNEDY
Arranged by DAN COATES

Say You'll Be There - 4 - 1

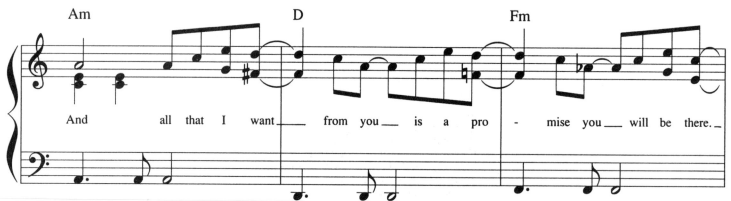

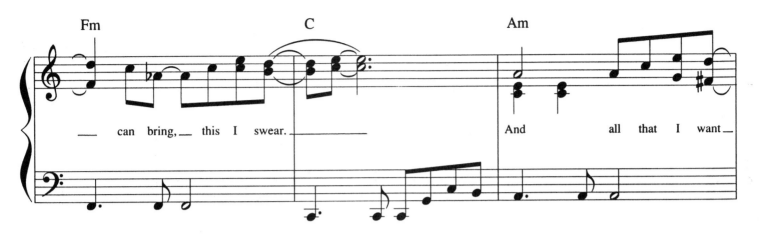

Verse 2:
If you put two and two together,
You will see what our friendship is for.
If you can't work out the equation
Then I guess I'll have to show you the door.
There is no need to say you love me,
It would be better left unsaid.

I'm giving you everything,
All that joy can bring,
This I swear.
And all that I want from you
Is a promise you will be there.

SEND ME A LOVER

Words and Music by
RICHARD HAHN and
GEORGE THATCHER
Arranged by DAN COATES

Send Me a Lover - 4 - 1

SET THE NIGHT TO MUSIC

Words and Music by
DIANE WARREN
Arranged by DAN COATES

Additional Lyrics

Let's find a rhythm all our own,
Melt into it nice and slow.
Love ourselves away from here.
Your heart beating next to mine,
Perfect love in perfect time.
Watch the world just disappear.
The moment is ours to take,
And with the love we make
We could.... (to Chorus)

SOMEBODY'S CRYING

Words and Music by
CHRIS ISAAK
Arranged by DAN COATES

1. I know some-bod-y and they cry for you.___
2. I know some-bod-y and they called your name___

They lie a-wake at night and dream of you.___ I bet you nev-er e-ven
a mil-lion times and still you nev-er came.___ They go on lov-ing you

know they do,___ but some-bod-y's cry-in'.
just the same.___ I know that some-bod-y's try-in'.

So

Somebody's Crying - 3 - 1

318

Somebody's Crying - 3 - 2

Verse 3:
Give me a sign and let me know we're through,
If you don't love me like I love you.
But if you cry at night the way I do,
I'll know that somebody's lyin'.

SOMETHING HAPPENED
ON THE WAY TO HEAVEN

Words and Music by
PHIL COLLINS and
DARYL STUERMER
Arranged by DAN COATES

Brightly (♩ = 120)

1.4. We had a life, we had a love,

but you don't know what you've got 'til you lose it.

Well, that was then and this is now, and I want you back.

Something Happened on the Way to Heaven - 4 - 1

322

you, you know_ I'd ___ I'd rath-er leave it.

me.

Extra Lyrics:

2. How can something so good, go so bad,
   How can something so right, go so wrong,
   I don't know, I don't have all the answers,
   But I want you back,
   How many times can I say I'm sorry?

3. I only wanted you as someone to love,
   But something happened on the way to heaven,
   It got a hold of me, and wouldn't let go,
   And I want you back,
   How many times can I say I'm sorry?

SOMETHING TO TALK ABOUT

Words and Music by
SHIRLEY EIKHARD
Arranged by DAN COATES

Moderate beat

Peo - ple are talk - ing,   talk - ing 'bout peo - ple.
I feel so fool - ish,   I nev - er no - ticed.

I hear them whis - per,   you won't be - lieve it.
You'd act so ner - vous,   could you be fall - ing for me?

Something to Talk about - 4 - 1

Lyrics: Let's give them some-thing to talk____ a - bout. How a - bout love?____

From the Lucasfilm Ltd. Productions "STAR WARS", "THE EMPIRE STRIKES BACK"
and "RETURN OF THE JEDI" - Twentieth Century-Fox Releases.

STAR WARS
(Main Theme)

Music by
JOHN WILLIAMS
Arranged by DAN COATES

Star Wars - 2 - 1

THE SWEETEST DAYS

Words and Music by
WENDY WALDMAN, JON LIND
and PHIL GALDSTON
Arranged by DAN COATES

TOO LATE, TOO SOON

Words and Music by
JON SECADA, JAMES HARRIS III
and TERRY LEWIS
Arranged by DAN COATES

334

Verse 2:
I wish I would have known,
I wouldn't have left you all alone.
Temptation led you wrong.
Tell me how long this has been goin' on?
'Cause I thought our love was strong,
But I guess I must be dreamin'.
(To Chorus:)

TAKE A BOW

Words and Music by
MADONNA CICCONE and BABYFACE
Arranged by DAN COATES

Take a bow, ___ the night is o - ver, this mas - que - rade ___ is

Make them laugh, ___ it comes so eas - y when you get to the part ___ where you're

Take a Bow - 4 - 1

TEARS IN HEAVEN

Words and Music by
WILL JENNINGS and ERIC CLAPTON
Arranged by DAN COATES

Moderately slow ♩ = 80

p legato

(with pedal)

G   D/F#   Em   G/D   C/E   G/D

mp

1. Would you know   my name____   if I   saw you in heav-
2. Would you hold   my hand____   if I   saw you in heav-

D   G/D D⁷   G   D/F#   Em   G/D

en?
en?   Would it be   the same____
Would you help   me stand____

C/E   G/D   D   G/D D⁷   Em

if I   saw you in heav-   en?
if I   saw you in heav-   en?   I must   be
I'll find   my

Tears in Heaven - 4 - 1

Tears in Heaven - 4 - 4

From the Twentieth Century-Fox Motion Picture

THAT THING YOU DO!

Words and Music by
ADAM SCHLESINGER
Arranged by DAN COATES

That Thing You Do! - 4 - 1

Verse 2:
I know all the games you play.
And I'm gonna find a way to let you know
That you'll be mine someday.
'Cause we could be happy, can't you see?
If you'd only let me be the one to hold you
And keep you here with me.
'Cause I try and try to forget you, girl,
But it's just too hard to do.
Every time you do that thing you do.

Verse 3:
(8 Bar Instrumental Solo...)
'Cause we could be happy, can't you see?
If you'd only let me be the one to hold you
And keep you here with me.
'Cause it hurts me so just to see you go
Around with someone new.
(To Coda:)

Theme from
LOVE AFFAIR

Music by
ENNIO MORRICONE
Arranged by DAN COATES

Theme from Love Affair - 2 - 1

TIME, LOVE AND TENDERNESS

Words and Music by
DIANE WARREN
Arranged by DAN COATES

Moderate, steady beat

So you say that you can't go on, love left you cry - in'.
I un-der-stand how you're feel-ing now, and what you've been through.

And you say all your hope is gone, and what's the use in try - in'.
But your world's gon - na turn a - round, so ba - by, don't you be blue.

What you need is to have some faith, shake off those sad blues.
All it takes is a lit - tle time to make it bet - ter.

Time, Love and Tenderness - 4 - 1

Get your self a new view, oh.
The hurt won't last for-ev - er, oh.
Noth-ing is as sad as it seems,_
All the tears are all gon-na dry,_

_ you know, 'cause
_ you know, 'cause
some-day you'll laugh at the heart-ache,

some-day you'll laugh at the pain.
Some-how you'll get through the heart-break,
You may be down on your luck but,

some-how you can get through the rain._
ba - by, that old luck's gon - na change._
When love

Time, Love and Tenderness - 4 - 4

UN-BREAK MY HEART

Words and Music by
DIANE WARREN
Arranged by DAN COATES

Un-Break My Heart - 5 - 1

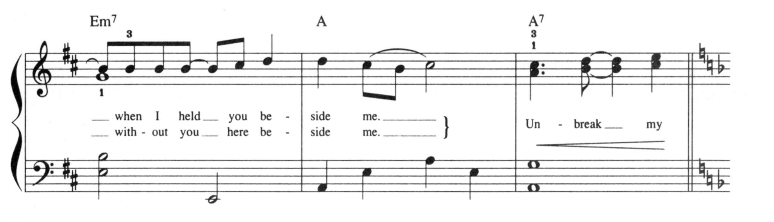

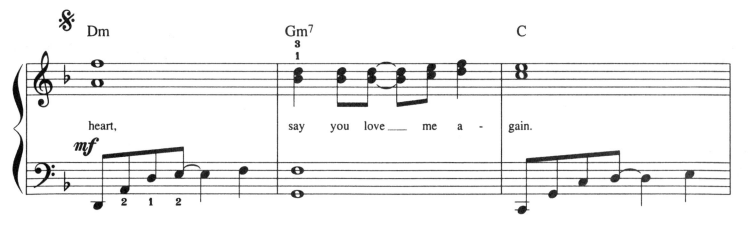

358

UNTIL I FIND YOU AGAIN

Music and Lyrics by
RICHARD MARX
Arranged by DAN COATES

Moderately slow ♩ = 78

mp legato

G
1. Late - ly I've been try - ing   to fill up my days __ since you're
2. The arms of hope sur - round __ me. Will time be a fair __ weath - er

F

C

(simile)

G
gone.
friend?
The speed of love is blind - ing   and I
Should I call out to an - gels   or just

F

C
did - n't know how __ to hold on. My mind __ won't clear, __ I'm out __
drink my - self sob - er a - gain? I can't hide __ this truth, __ I still burn __

G

Am

Until I Find You Again - 3 - 1

Until I Find You Again - 3 - 3

VALENTINE

Composed by
JIM BRICKMAN and JACK KUGELL
Arranged by DAN COATES

Valentine - 4 - 1

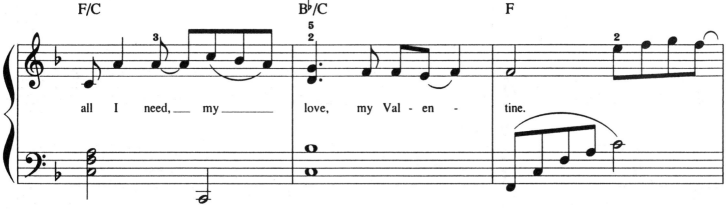

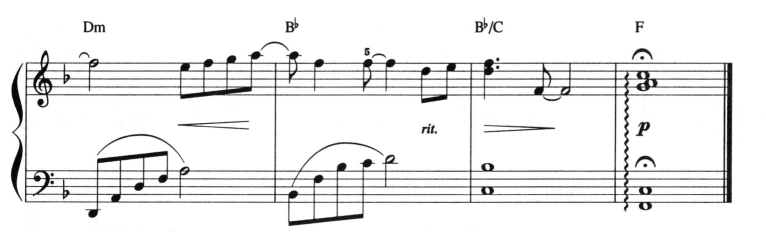

Verse 2:
All of my life,
I have been waiting for all you give to me.
You've opened my eyes
And shown me how to love unselfishly.
I've dreamed of this a thousand times before,
But in my dreams I couldn't love you more.
I will give you my heart until the end of time.
You're all I need, my love,
My Valentine.

WHEN I SEE YOU SMILE

Words and Music by
DIANE WARREN
Arranged by DAN COATES

Moderately, with expression (♩ = 69)

When I See You Smile - 6 - 1

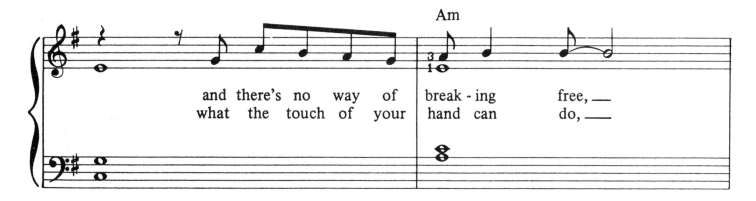

When I see you smile, _____ yeah, I can face the world. Oh, _____ you know I can do an-y-thing now. When I see you smile, _____ oh yeah,_ ba-by, when I see you_ smile.

Smile at _____ me.

WHEN YOU TELL ME THAT YOU LOVE ME

Words and Music by
ALBERT HAMMOND and JOHN BETTIS
Arranged by DAN COATES

When You Tell Me That You Love Me - 5 - 4

From the Original Motion Picture Soundtrack "BEACHES"

THE WIND BENEATH MY WINGS

Words and Music by
LARRY HENLEY and JEFF SILBAR
Arranged by DAN COATES

The Wind beneath My Wings - 5 - 1

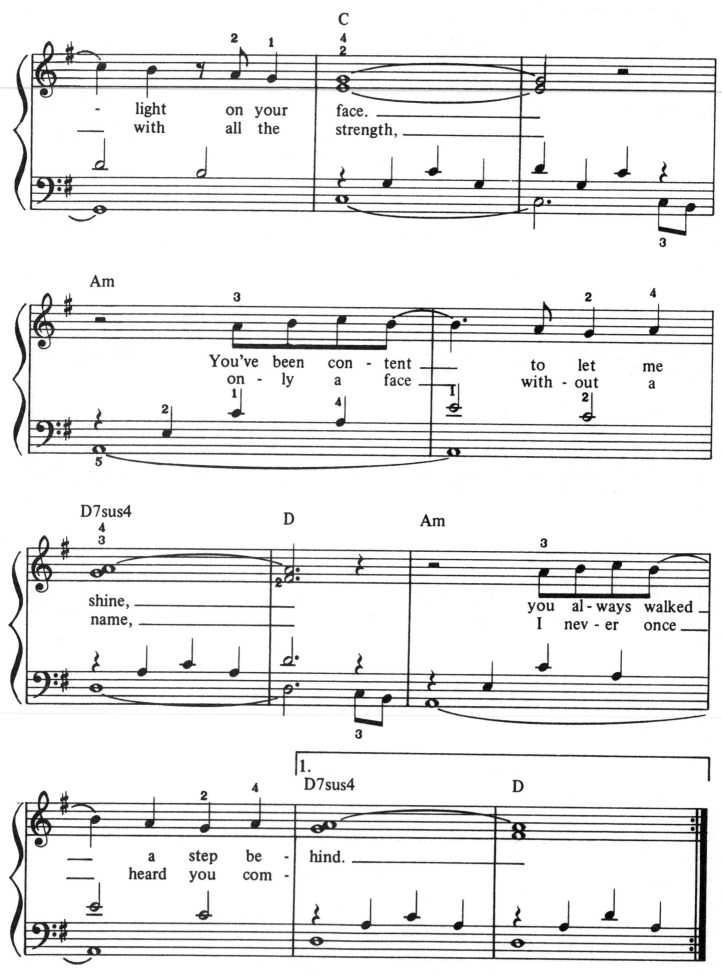

The Wind beneath My Wings - 5 - 2

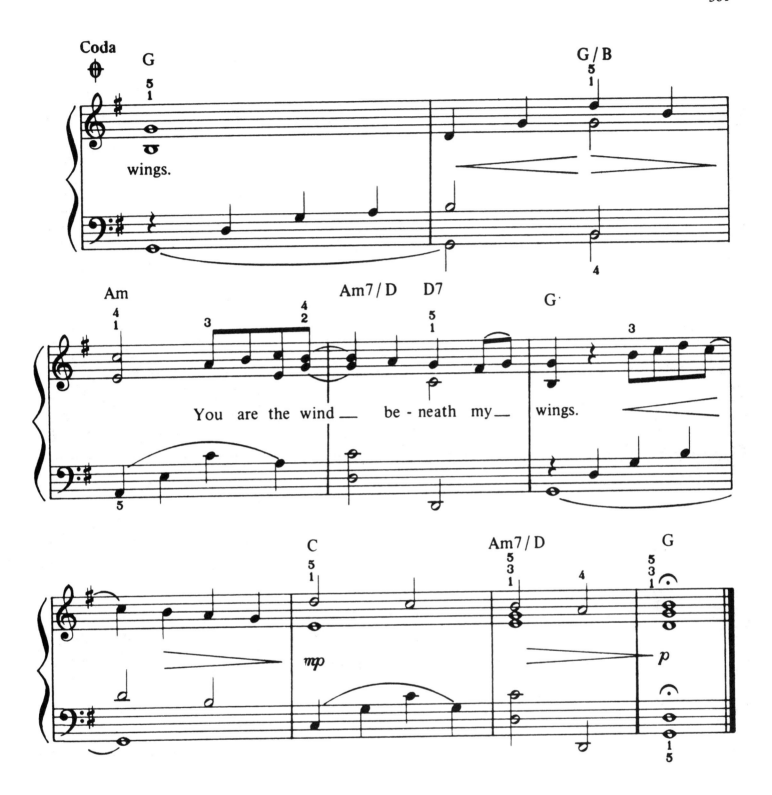

3. It might have appeared to go unnoticed
that I've got it all here in my heart.
I want you to know I know the truth:
I would be nothing without you.

WILL YOU BE THERE
(Theme from ''Free Willy'')

Written and Composed by
MICHAEL JACKSON
Arranged by DAN COATES

Hold me_____ like the Riv - er Jor - dan, and I will then
wear - y_____ tell me will you hold me, when wrong, will you

say to thee when you are my friend._____
scold me, when lost will you find me? But they

Car - ry me, like you are my broth - er. Love me like a
told me a man should be faith - ful and walk when not

Will You Be There - 4 - 2

385

Will You Be There - 4 - 4

YOU ARE NOT ALONE

Written and Composed by
R. KELLY
Arranged by DAN COATES

388

You Are Not Alone - 5 - 3

YOU WERE MEANT FOR ME

Words and Music by
JEWEL KILCHER and STEVE POLTZ
Arranged by DAN COATES

Moderate swing feel

I hear the clock, it's six A. M.,

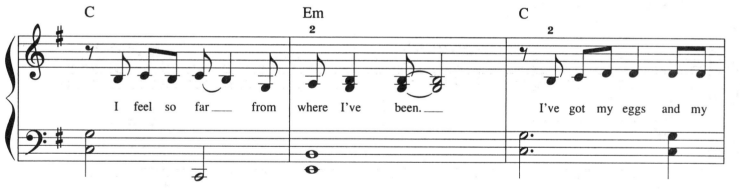

I feel so far___ from where I've been.___ I've got my eggs and my

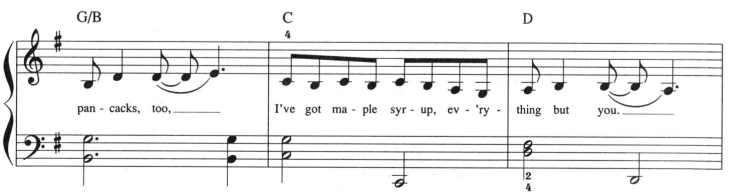

pan-cacks, too,_____ I've got ma-ple syr-up, ev-'ry- thing but you.

You Were Meant for Me - 5 - 1

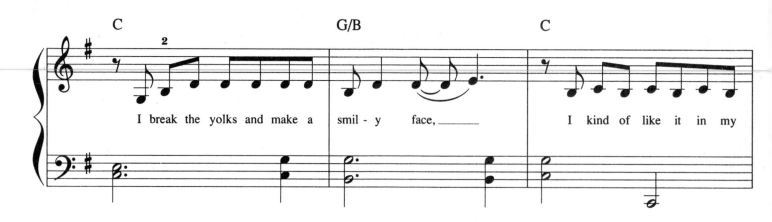

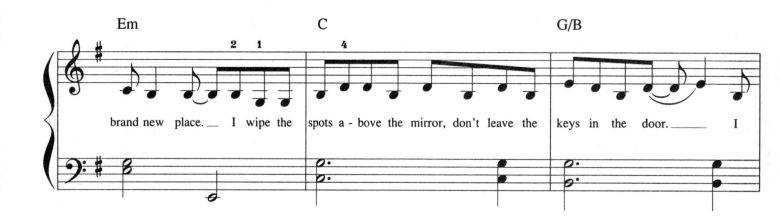

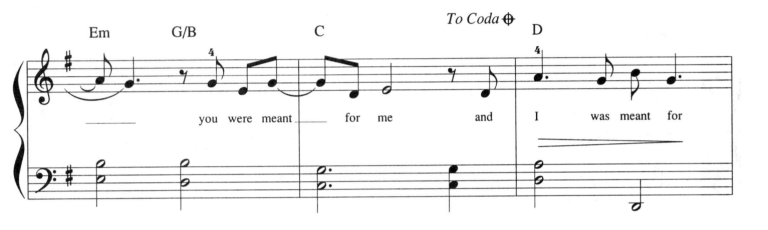

You Were Meant for Me - 5 - 3

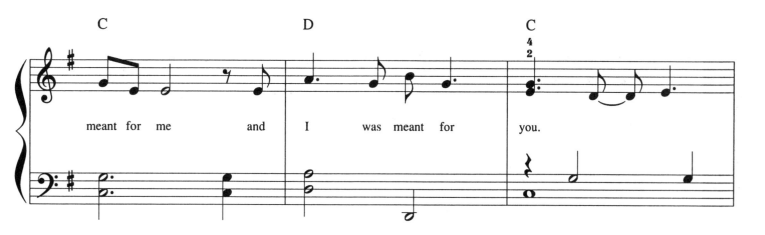

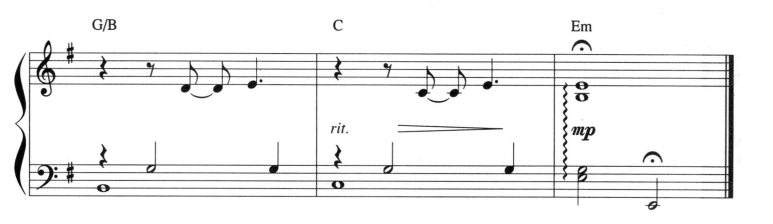

Verse 2:
I called my mama, she was out for a walk.
Consoled a cup of coffee, but it didn't wanna talk.
So I picked up a paper, it was more bad news,
More hearts being broken or people being used.
Put on my coat in the pouring rain.
I saw a movie, it just wasn't the same,
'Cause it was happy and I was sad,
And it made me miss you, oh, so bad.
(To Chorus:)

Verse 3:
I brush my teeth and put the cap back on,
I know you hate it when I leave the light on.
I pick a book up and then I turn the sheets down,
And then I take a breath and a good look around.
Put on my pj's and hop into bed.
I'm half alive but I feel mostly dead.
I try and tell myself it'll be all right,
I just shouldn't think anymore tonight.
(To Chorus:)

YOU GOT IT

Words and Music by
ROY ORBISON, TOM PETTY
and JEFF LYNNE
Arranged by DAN COATES

Moderately slow ♩ = 88

legato

mp

Ev - 'ry time I look in - to your love - ly
Ev - 'ry time I hold you, I be - gin to un - der -

mp

eyes,
stand.

I see a love that
Ev - 'ry - thing a - bout you

mon - ey just can't buy.
tells me you're my man.

cresc.

One
I

You Got It - 4 - 1

398

You Got It - 4 - 3

YOU MEAN THE WORLD TO ME

Words and Music by
L.A. REID, DARYL SIMMONS
and BABYFACE
Arranged by DAN COATES

Moderate, steady beat

If you could give me one good rea - son
gon - na take some work - in' but

why I should be - lieve___ you, be lieve in all the -things that you tell.___
I be - lieve you're worth it, as long as your in - ten - tions are good.___

I would sure like to be - lieve you, my
There is just one way to show it and

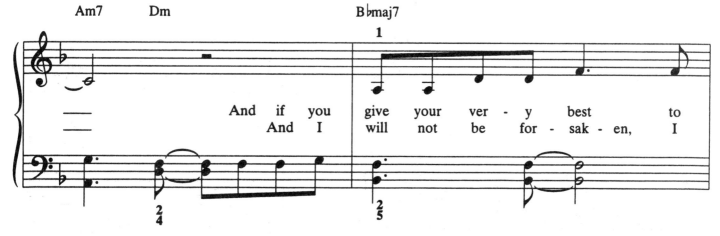

YOU'LL SEE

Words and Music by
MADONNA CICCONE and
DAVID FOSTER
Arranged by DAN COATES

You'll See - 4 - 1

Verse 2:
You think that I can never laugh again,
You'll see.
You think that you've destroyed my faith in love.
You think after all you've done,
I'll never find my way back home.
You'll see, somehow, some day.   *(To Chorus:)*

Verse 3:
You think that you are strong, but you are weak,
You'll see.
It takes more strength to cry, admit defeat.
I have truth on my side,
You only have deceit.
You'll see, somehow, some day.   *(To Chorus:)*

FROM A DISTANCE

Lyrics and Music by
JULIE GOLD

Arranged by DAN COATES

dis - tance, the world looks blue and green, and the snow - capped moun - tains white. From a dis - tance, the o - cean meets the stream, and the ea - gle takes to flight. From a dis - tance there is

From a Distance - 4 - 1

From a Distance - 4 - 3

Verse 2:
From a distance, we all have enough
And no one is in need.
There are no guns, no bombs, no diseases,
No hungry mouths to feed.
From a distance, we are instruments
Marching in a common band;
Playing songs of hope, playing songs of peace,
They're the songs of every man.

Verse 3:
From a distance, you look like my friend
Even though we are at war.
From a distance, I just cannot comprehend
What all this fighting is for.
From a distance, there is harmony
And it echoes through the land.
It's the hope of hopes. It's the love of loves.
It's the heart of every man.

FOREVER'S AS FAR AS I'LL GO

Words and Music by
MIKE REID
Arranged by DAN COATES

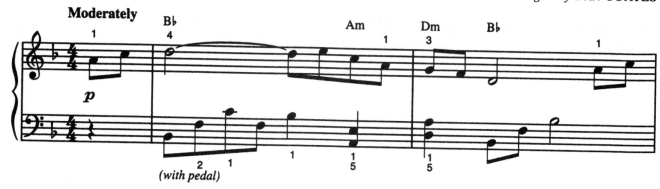

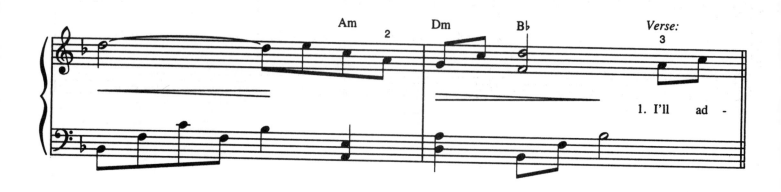

1. I'll ad-mit I could feel__ it the first time that we touched. The look in your eyes__

said you felt as much.__ But I'm not a man who falls so eas - i - ly.

Forever's As Far As I'll Go - 3 - 1

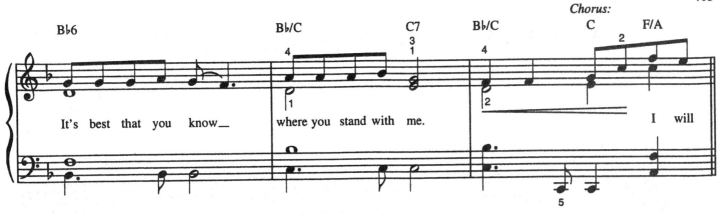

It's best that you know___ where you stand with me. I will

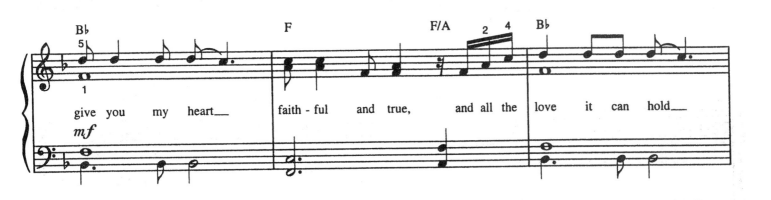

give you my heart___ faith-ful and true, and all the love it can hold___

that's all I can do. But I've thought a-bout___ how long I'll love you,

and it's on-ly fair___ that you know___ for-ev-er's as far as I'll___

Forever's As Far As I'll Go - 3 - 2

416

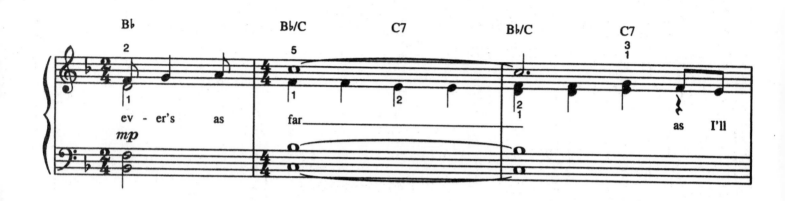

Verse 2:
When there's age around my eyes and gray in your hair,
And it only takes a touch to recall the love we've shared.
I won't take for granted that you know my love is true.
Each night in your arms, I will whisper to you...
(To Chorus:)